SONGS MY MOTHER

SANG TO ME

PATRICIA PRECIADO MARTIN

Songs My Mother
❧ *Sang to Me* ❧

AN ORAL HISTORY OF
MEXICAN AMERICAN WOMEN

The University of Arizona Press
Tucson

Fifth printing 1998
The University of Arizona Press
Copyright © 1992
Arizona Board of Regents
All Rights Reserved

02 01 00 99 98   9 8 7 6 5

LIBRARY OF CONGRESS CATALOGING-IN-PUBLICATION DATA

Martin, Patricia Preciado.
   Songs my mother sang to me : an oral history of
Mexican American women / Patricia Preciado Martin.
      p.   cm.
   Includes index.
   ISBN 0-8165-1279-5 (cloth : acid-free paper). —
   ISBN 0-8165-1329-5 (pbk : acid-free paper)
   1. Mexican American women—Folklore.   2. Oral
tradition—Arizona.   3. Oral tradition—Mexico—Sonora
(State).   4. Arizona—Social life and customs.   5. Sonora
(Mexico : State)—Social life and customs.   I. Title.
GR111.M49M37   1992   92-6745
398'.0896872073—dc20   CIP

British Library Cataloguing-in-Publication Data
A catalogue record for this book is available from the British Library.

Dedicated to four

generations of Rascón women:

my maternal grandmother, Mercedes,

my mother, Aurelia,

and my sister and daughter,

Elena M. and Elena B.

Gracias a la vida
Que me ha dado tanto;
Me ha dado la marcha
De mis pies cansados;

Con ellos anduve
Ciudades y charcos,
Playas y desiertos,
Montañas y llanos,

Y la casa tuya,
Tu calle,
Y tu patio.

Gracias a la vida
Que me ha dado tanto
Me ha dado la risa
Me ha dado el llanto
Con ellos distingo
Dicho de quebranto
Que es el canto de Uds.
Que es mi mismo canto
Que es el canto de todos
Que es mi propio canto.*

*This song, "Gracias A La Vida," is by Violeta Parra.

Contents

Illustrations

Foreword

Since the eighteenth century, Spanish-speaking peoples have lived off the soil in the remote canyons and valleys of Southern Arizona. In 1736 silver was discovered, but by the nineteenth century the region would be coveted for its copper. By 1910, Arizona had become "the nation's number one producer of copper."[1] Equally important, during the late nineteenth and early twentieth centuries, family farms dotted the landscape. Relying on a mixed economy of livestock and subsistence crops, Mexican homesteaders created communities out of isolation. Kin and friendship networks spanned the artificial border separating Arizona from Sonora.

The ten women profiled here articulate daily rhythms, expectations, and cultural practices that no longer exist. Mining towns lie in ruins, and dude ranches, subdivisions, and corporate agriculture have replaced the family-run homesteads. Having a deep sense of their own heritage and connection to the land, some families, like the Salazars and Wilbur-Cruces, retained a small portion of their holdings as their own historical marker, as a place to hold reunions and other important family gatherings. The voices you will hear in *Songs My Mother Sang to Me* speak of the passing of distinct ways of life; yet the women's words hold neither anger nor bitterness. Their memories preserve both a rich Mexican-American agrarian tradition as well as a sense of neighborhood ties in segregated mining towns. But most of the women also made a transition from *el rancho al barrio*, from the ranch to Tucson. These women are the daughters of ranchers, cowhands, boarding-house keepers, laundresses, and midwives. As young children, they tended cattle and people. They also participated in a calendar of social events where religion played an instrumental role in fostering community ties and forging cultural identity.[2]

Songs My Mother Sang to Me broadens our understanding of Mexican American history. Representing one of the few studies focusing on Arizona, on rural life,[3] and on the transition from rural to urban, this collection provides an important counterpoint to the largely urban (and California/Texas) orientation of contemporary Chicano scholarship. Women, moreover, take center stage. One sees their history through their eyes. Lavish in detail and emotion, the ten narratives move beyond nostalgic renditions of daily life; they offer glimpses into women's relationship to the land and to the means of production. Gender roles, community building, and cultural resiliency appear as the major threads running through each interview. Patricia Preciado Martin introduces us to ten individual personalities and experiences; yet, these women share a deep appreciation of their culture and communities. Most are superb storytellers. One can almost taste the chicken with pumpkin seeds and visualize the home altar lovingly decorated with dime-store trinkets.

This volume also begins the process of identifying Mexican women's relationship to nature. Both in her memoir, *A Beautiful, Cruel Country*,[4] and her oral history included here, Eva Antonia Wilbur-Cruce evoked images of a girlhood filled with prairie dogs, roadrunners, and a Mexican hawk who flew away whenever she sang. In tending a water hole miles from her home, she made friends with the animals and the landscape. Recalling how she laid down to rest across a branch of an old oak tree, she declared, "I felt some sort of nutrition coming from the tree . . . it gave me the stamina that I didn't have."

Contemplating the natural world, however, was a coveted luxury. Whether from a ranching or mining family, daughters were expected to perform a round of arduous chores. The labor of female kin, regardless of age, proved instrumental in ensuring the family's economic survival. Women preserved food for the winter, sold surplus commodities to neighbors, did laundry for Anglo employers, and provided homes for lodgers. They also herded livestock, milked cows, built fences, and harvested crops. A strict division of labor according to gender became blurred, particularly with daughters of working men. Yet, this seemingly egalitarian assignment of tasks in no way subverted the traditional notion of "woman's place." Before the break of dawn, Rosalía Salazar Whelan would rise to gather kindling, milk the cows, and afterwards walk several miles to school, a routine which began with serving her father a cup of coffee. Elders closely regulated the activities of youth at work and at leisure. Young women were chaperoned during dances and other community social events. The parents of Livia León Montiel instructed Livia's visiting suitor (and future husband) to join them as they knelt to recite the family rosary. "It was a real education for him to be told that it was rosary time."

The family served as the locus of production with each member contributing her or his share. While the days of ranchers' and miners' wives never seemed to end, their economic situation became even more precarious when widowed or abandoned. The narratives of Esperanza Montoya Padilla and Julia Yslas Vélez poignantly describe the lives of single mothers. With courage, fortitude, and faith, they relied on their domestic skills to feed their children. Julia Yslas Vélez recalled how her mother, who came from a middle-class background in Mexico, peddled her handmade garments to "poor" Mexicanos: "She did not have a formal education, but she was very smart. She had a little book. . . . She used to mark in it what people owed her. She would draw a circle for a dollar and a half circle for fifty cents." Historians have often overlooked Mexican women's participation in the informal economy; however, these narratives clearly demonstrate the importance and variety of their work. Furthermore, women, as healers (curanderas) and midwives (parteras), nurtured the networks essential for building communities.

A layering of generations and peoples characterized rural Arizona. Mexicano migrants from Sonora homesteaded alongside native-born Mexican Americans. Marriages occurred across generational and racial lines. Boarding houses brought people together. At Josefa's Boarding House in Superior, for instance, a young Sonoran miner successfully courted Josefa's Arizona-born daughter. The oral histories that follow reveal the social and biological mixing of Indians, Spaniards, Mexicans, and Anglos. As an example, Rosalía Salazar was the child of a Mexican mother and a "full-blooded Opata Indian" father. She married Wilford Whelan, whose mother Ignacia was Mexicana. This multiracial society extended beyond two or three groups. The reader catches glimpses of the Chinese grocer, the African-American woman healer, and the Greek owner of a candy store. Yet, these interviews evidence the development of a distinctly Mexican-American agrarian culture, one which incorporated those willing to partake of it. Some "Americanos" attended fiestas, dances, and religious pageants. Assimilation was not a one-way street. In Southern Arizona, assimilation seemed to be thrown in reverse. Intermarriage did not guarantee the anglicization of the region's Spanish-speaking peoples. "Many of the offspring of Mexican-Anglo unions emphasized their Mexican rather than their Anglo heritage," observed historian Thomas Sheridan. "The reasons they did so testify to the enduring strength of Mexican society in the face of Anglo political and economic hegemony."[5] Indeed, the voices in this volume point to the existence (at least in Southern Arizona) of an expansive Mexican cultural horizon where one's "positionality" or identity rested not in some essentialist biological mooring but through acceptance and adoption of Mexican cultural values and expectations.

While these narratives tend to emphasize community bonds and mutual interests, they also record instances of racial and gender discrimination. Several women mentioned the lack of formal education because of segregated schools and uncaring teachers. In the words of Paulina Moreno Montoya: "I went to school in Redington when there were teachers, but they often never lasted more than a month—just long enough to go back on the next supply wagon." She elaborated further, "All the teachers . . . were Americanas, but since I only spoke Spanish," and "I never did learn English . . . I guess I lost interest because school was so off and on." "I'll admit there was a lot of discrimination in those years," declared Carlotta Silvas Martin as she explained the division of Superior, Arizona, into "American" and "Mexican" sides of town. More dramatically, Esperanza Montoya Padilla vividly recounted the fear she felt as she, her recently widowed mother, and her siblings were forced to abandon the family-run boarding house in the face of systematic harassment and terror. In the dark of night, someone kept turning the doorknob and separating the vines from the window. Reaching a point of desperation, her mother "just took the clothes for the three of us and left everything." She continued, "After we left, whoever it was did a good job of robbing us. They took everything—dishes, jewelry, furniture—anything of value, even the *santos*."

To meet the physical and psychological challenges (and downright assaults), Mexican women drew upon their cultural traditions for faith, strength, and identity. The women profiled here did not view Catholicism as an institution of oppression. Rather, religious practices permeated everyday routines. In preparing the masa for tortillas, the mother of Virginia Gastelum "would always add salt to the flour in the form of *la Santa Cruz* (the Holy Cross)—*para bendecir la masa* (to bless the dough). Many of the interviewees can still recite childhood rhymes, prayers, and songs. Socorro Delgado can recall by heart the family prayers offered at Christmas, supplications made in front of an elaborate nativity scene. Home altars symbolized in a literal sense how people created their own expressions of religious belief. Each family had their own special saints and feast days, often originating as remembrances for favors granted. El día de San Juan (June 24th) and Christmas brought together entire communities. Las Posadas, a pageant in which residents gathered in a procession from house to house, affirmed the practice of ritualized visiting among kin and friends. It seemed as much a celebration of community networks as a religious journey. From a small home altar nestled atop a bureau dresser to a well-orchestrated town play or pageant, Mexicans of Southern Arizona viewed their own interpretations of Catholicism as integral parts of their cultural life. The stories in this volume illuminate a rich, distinctive border culture, one which placed high value on family bonds, religious faith, and communal identity.

Themes of family and community dominate the narratives. The ten women of *Songs My Mother Sang to Me* present their experiences not as texts of individual struggles but as pieces of communal histories. They situate themselves within the context of Mexican agrarian life in Southern Arizona. With a twinge of nostalgia, they look back on a world that now exists only in their memories. The connection between physical and cultural roots remains strong. Livia León Montiel explained the importance of reunions on the family homestead as follows: "The only way you can hold your family together is by uniting with them from time to time. Today everybody lives in a different place—we are all so scattered. . . . If it would only be possible for them to hold on to this little piece of land for all of them to reunite. . . . This is my hope and my legacy." I invite you now to meet these women, each with her own story to tell but all sharing in the rich cultural traditions of Mexican Arizona.   VICKI L. RUIZ

NOTES

1. Thomas Sheridan, *Los Tucsonenses: The Mexican Community in Tucson, 1854–1941* (Tucson: University of Arizona Press, 1986), pp. 13–15; James E. Officer, *Hispanic Arizona, 1536–1856* (Tucson: University of Arizona Press, 1987), p. 4; Rodolfo Acuña, *Occupied America: A History of Chicanos*, 2nd ed. (New York: Harper and Row, 1981), p. 89.

2. Thomas Sheridan in *Los Tucsonenses* discusses this interplay of religion and agrarian traditions. See pages 159–63.

3. In addition to the previously cited works, Patricia Preciado Martin's *Images and Conversations: Mexican Americans Recall a Southwestern Past* (Tucson: University of Arizona Press, 1983) and Raquel Rubio Goldsmith's "Shipwrecked in the Desert: A Short History of the Mexican Sisters of the House of the Providence in Douglas, Arizona, 1927–1949," in *Women on the U.S.–Mexico Border*, eds. Vicki L. Ruiz and Susan Tiano (Winchester, MA: Allen and Unwin, 1987, rpt. by Westview Press, 1991) addresses the historical experiences of Arizona Mexicans. Other works which examine Mexican-American rural traditions include Sarah Deutsch's *No Separate Refuge: Culture, Class, and*

Gender on an Anglo-Hispanic Frontier in the American Southwest, 1880–1940 (New York: Oxford University Press, 1987) and Nan Elasasser, et. al., *Las Mujeres: Conversations with the Hispanic Community* (Old Westbury: Feminist Press, 1980).

4. Eva Antonia Wilbur-Cruce, *A Beautiful Cruel Country* (Tucson: University of Arizona Press, 1990).

5. Sheridan, *Los Tucsonenses*, p. 147.

Preface

El que vive en el recuerdo nunca muere.
The person who is remembered never dies.

The invitation read: To the descendants and relatives of Epimenio and Crespina Salazar.

Dear Family and Friends,
Con el favor de Dios we would like to join together to have our family reunion. For some, it might be our last. For some, it has been many years since we have seen each other. Let's not let anything stand in our way and make our re-union a fun-filled, happy, and memorable event. We need everyone's cooperation to make it so. The celebration will be held in Aravaipa Canyon on September 1, 1990, in honor of Rosalía Salazar Whelan. The mass will be held in the family church at noon. There will be softball, horse-shoes, volleyball, gunnysack races and piñatas. A barbecue dinner will be served at 4:00 P.M. and dancing will begin at sundown with music by Los Amigos. See you there!

Nothing could have prepared me for that event. The trip itself was an unforgettable journey of the spirit—a three-hour drive from Tucson to the remoteness of the Aravaipa Canyon Wilder-ness—part of it through some of the most beautiful and isolated country in the Southwest. The farmland and fruit orchards of the Sulphur Springs Valley north of Willcox gave way to huge expanses of windswept grasslands interspersed with isolated ranches, flowering yucca trees, and creaking windmills. The blue wildness of the Graham Mountains was scarved with the woolly black clouds of the late summer monsoons. Elsewhere the light was brilliant, the sky azure. Red-tailed hawks peppered the horizon, riding the wind drafts as carelessly and joyously as leaves.

In time the mountain-rimmed valley narrowed, and the sheer red and gold cliffs of El Cañón rose gradually above a clear and perennial stream. Half-hidden and abandoned adobe homes beside the twisting dirt road were sheltered by enormous cottonwood and sycamore trees.

Soon the Salazar family chapel—once the home of Epimenio and Crespina Salazar and their family of eight children—came into view. Its venerable adobe walls were filled to overflowing with their descendants as well as the descendants of many of the other families that had once called this wilderness outpost their home. Some stood outside in groups, their heads bowed reverently, as the prayers of the mass, the guitar music, and the hymns of the faithful wafted through the open windows and doors of the *capilla* into the humid summer air.

And then the songs drifted down a short stretch of the narrow road and up a rocky incline overlooking the cliffs of El Cañón to the Salazar family cemetery, where surely they stirred the rejoicing spirits that rested there.

After mass the invited streamed to the fallow creekside fields that lay a short distance from the chapel and set up camp under the sheltering trees. Campfire smoke rose like an offering up the steep sunlit walls of El Cañón, and the ancient orchard that once bore fruit now bore witness.

There were tents, motorhomes, trucks, and trailers. Children played tag and shouted in delight at the piñatas. Adults greeted one another and embraced and exchanged news. Young couples strolled arm in arm under the huge green canopies of the trees. Rosalía Salazar Whelan, the guest of honor, sat with others of her generation in folding chairs, reminiscing and keeping vigil. Birds sang; dogs barked; roosters crowed; the creekside cattle lowed; the rooftop peacocks screamed.

The delicious smell of *barbacoa* filled the air and the guests—now more than three hundred strong—stood in line to be served. At dusk the music began, and young and old alike danced into the night on a crowded wooden platform. The band played on and on, and the revelers added their *gritos* of jubilation to the profusion of songs that now ascended into the starlit canyon night. They were the songs of brotherhood and sisterhood, of community and roots and connection, of culture and tradition, of birth and death, of permanence and change, of work and leisure, of struggle and sorrow, of struggle and survival, of tragedy and triumph. And most of all, they were the songs of reunion and remembrance.

The Salazar family celebration in Aravaipa Canyon, a historical and exuberant happening, parallels in many ways the concept and creation of this book. I "discovered" Rosalía Salazar Whelan, one of the subjects of my interviews, while reading the obituary notice of her sister, Victoria Salazar Tapia, in a Tucson newspaper. The article, which included a biography of Victoria's long and active life—she died just before her eightieth birthday—announced her funeral in the Salazar family chapel in remote Aravaipa Canyon two hundred miles northeast of Tucson. The list of her survivors included one sibling, Rosalía Salazar Whelan, who now resided in Patagonia, a small ranching and retirement community in Southern Arizona near the Mexican border.

A few weeks later, while visiting the Santa Cruz Valley south of Tucson in search of potential interviewees for my book, I met Edilia Rodriguez, the postmistress of Tumacácori who, as it turned out, was related to Sra. Whelan. Our chance conversation led me to make a phone call to Margaret Salge, a daughter of Sra. Whelan, who also lives in Patagonia. I explained that I was interested in conducting oral history interviews in order to document the lives and recollections of Mexican-American women of her mother's generation. She responded enthusiastically, and Sra. Whelan agreed to an interview. A short time later I completed the first of two interviews with Sra. Whelan at the kitchen table in her tree-shaded adobe home along the banks of a creek in the foothills of Patagonia.

Other interviews followed. I relied on networking, personal and professional references, determination, just plain luck, and as in the case of Rosalía Salazar Whelan, not a small assortment of miracles and coincidences: Julia Yslas Vélez and Livia León Montiel are the mothers of personal friends; Eva Antonia Wilbur-Cruce was introduced to me by Pat Shelton, an editor at the University of Arizona Press; I met Paulina Moreno Montoya while going door to door (with my heart in my mouth) in the small historical community of Tubac; a young woman filming a documentary on miners called me for a reference, and in turn referred me to her future mother-in-law, Esperanza Montoya Padilla; Cecelia Esquer, a Phoenix attorney, told me about Carlotta Silvas Martin; I called Socorro Félix Delgado to obtain a phone number of a possible lead. And the rest, as the saying goes, is history.

I had several criteria in mind while selecting the subjects for my interviews. First and foremost, I wished to document the lives and memories of the women of my mother's and grandmothers' eras, before they were lost or forgotten—like those of so many generations of Mexican-American women before them—to the passage of time, benign forgetfulness, and the fast-paced changes of modern life.

Secondly, I was interested in documenting as varied an experience of the contributions of Mexican-American women as possible, being all too painfully aware of the negative stereotypes of Mexicana women that cinema, television, and popular Western literature so relentlessly and callously pursue. I was interested in the total mosaic, not only of the individual's life, but in the history and traditions that she might pass on. To that end I traveled to ranching and mining towns and to rural as well as urban areas to conduct my interviews. Like the Salazar family reunion, the result was unexpected and exuberant, for the manuscript contains a surprisingly wide spectrum of the Mexican-American woman's experiences. There are farmers and ranchers, cooks and midwives, healers and businesswomen, poets and musicians, spiritual leaders and actresses, teachers and journalists, seamstresses and artists, political leaders and laundresses, to name but a few.

Finally, I was guided by the certain knowledge that the history of the West and El Norte was chronicled by the male explorer, soldier, missionary priest, prospector, and warrior. If the history of this area has fallen short in documenting the histories of women in general, how much greater the void relating to the history of the Mexican-American pioneer woman of El Norte. Indeed, the very dearth of information indirectly guided the outcome of this book; like the wilderness of El Cañón, I had no boundaries, the territory was uncharted, and the horizon unlimited.

The interviews themselves were often preceded by a "get-acquainted" visit. Family members might be present while I explained the purpose of my project. The interviews were conducted in whatever language the interviewee felt most comfortable with: English or Spanish—and often a combination of the two—as is habitual with those of us who have been born and reared in the bilingual-bicultural environment of Arizona. The questions asked followed the same general outline: family and personal history and geneology, childhood memories, secular and religious traditions, education, work and leisure, environment and living conditions, rites of passage, and values. More often than not the direction of the interview struck its own course depending on the interests and personality of the woman being interviewed. As a result each chapter bears its own unique stamp of individuality and spontaneity. In subsequent visits and journeys with these women, whom I had now befriended, I took notes or carried a portable tape recorder in order to document any additional recollections that might be forthcoming. In the course of these narrations, it is important to keep in mind that these women document not only the rich details of their own lives, but also the histories of their ancestors, family, and communities, thus adding to the general store of knowledge of the culture, contributions, and abiding presence of the Mexican-American people in the Southwest.

The interviews were transcribed word for word and then edited for flow, continuity, and chronology. I retained all that was of historical, anecdotal, and human interest. Repetitions and conversation unrelated to the historical goals of the interview were deleted, and at all times I was respectful of the individuals' confidences. Transitional words were interjected when necessary to aid the flow of the text, and I completed the words to some of the songs that had been remembered only in part. But the body of each chapter, told in the first person, is true to the voice of the narrator. Each woman indeed shares "her song."

The expeditions, such as the one to Aravaipa Canyon, I undertook to better understand the circumstances and the poetry of these women's lives. I traveled to the boulder-strewn, abandoned mining town of Mascot; to the verdant mystery of Arivaca Creek; to the shrouded mesquite *bosques* of the San Pedro River Valley; to the isolated cemeteries of old settlements; and to the endless expanses of Redington Pass in El Rincón, where, in the words of Paulina Moreno Montoya, "the only place you could look was up; the only thing you could see were the stars."

The interviews and conversations themselves took place under the most prosaic of circumstances: tableside, bedside, chairside, roadside. But I never failed to be transported by the recollections of these women; they drew me into landscapes and dreamscapes as unforgettable and varied as the shining wilderness of El Cañón. They opened their doors and hearts to me; they sang their songs to me. I am still basking in the warmth of their patience and trust and generosity.

Might I add that I was drawn to them—am still drawn to them—as much for their past as for their vitality and connection to the present. The refrains of their histories will continue to play over and over again in the symphonies of our own lives. We can be but the richer and wiser for the music.

POSTSCRIPT

It has been difficult for me to write about this collection of oral history in objective and ordinary terms. This book was also motivated by very personal feelings—a love and respect for the richness and power of my Mexican heritage, and an abiding love for the memory of my maternal grandmother, Mercedes Rascón Romero. My Grandmother Mercedes, a *mestiza* of Tarahumara lineage, came to Clifton, Arizona, from Guerrero, Chihuahua, as a young bride in the late 1800s. She lived in El Barrio de los Alacranes in a home that my Grandfather Exiquio built. The house still stands where she bore and raised her children. She was tall—five feet and ten inches—and elegant. She was known for her beauty, her gentility, her spirituality, her generosity, her skill as a seamstress and cook, and her musical ability. She died during the harshness of the Depression years—some say of a broken heart—and is buried in what was once a segregated cemetery in Clark-dale, Arizona. I never knew her; she never sang her songs to me. Perhaps this is, in the final analysis, what sent me on this journey of the heart.   PATRICIA PRECIADO MARTIN

Acknowledgments

I am most indebted to my husband, Jim, without whose financial support this book would not have been possible. He underwrote my photographic and transcribing equipment and my typing and duplicating expenses. He financed my journeys (and ate canned corned beef in my absences) and tolerated my long hours at my desk and my sleepless nights. In the midst of it all he had the patience to review the manuscript and still take me out dancing once in a while. And *gracias* also to my sister, Elena, and her *tocaya* (namesake)—my daughter, Elena—who never failed to encourage me in my efforts. *Gracias también* to my *amiguita*, Belén Ramírez, who accompanied me on some of my adventures and cheered me with her *conversación* and *canciones*. *Mil gracias* to Norma Tapia Luepke, who carries on her family tradition in Aravaipa Canyon, and whose hospitality on my many visits there will not be forgotten. I am *muy agradecida* to my typist, Doris Strathdee, who tolerated last-minute changes and my own self-imposed hysterical deadlines. She also delivers! *Gracias también* to my church family—the Carrillos and Gallardos—whose historical standing and sterling connections put me in good stead with the community. And *gracias, mil gracias*, to all the beautiful women and their families who allowed me to share not only in their lives, but also in their love and at their table.

Livia León Montiel

M Y NAME IS LIVIA LEÓN MONTIEL. I was born on July
1, 1914, in Rillito, Arizona. The paternal side of my
family are the true Tucson pioneers. They were here
before Arizona became part of the United States. My great-
grandfather was present at the signing of the Gadsden Purchase
in 1853. His name was Francisco Solano León; his father, whose
name was José León, was here during the times of the Presidio,
or so I'm told. Francisco Solano León was a rancher—a cattle and
land baron, as he was called in those days. He had property
throughout Tucson and a ranch at the Baboquivari. It was a big
ranch, and my father said they used to go there in the summer; it
was where he kept most of his cattle. Out of that family there
were four daughters and three sons—Cirilo León was my grandfather. He was married to Eloisa Ferrer, and they had four children. My father, Luis, was the second born. Francisco Solano
León had a lot of land, and he gave all of his children a parcel.
The part that he gave to my grandfather is where El Río Golf
Course is now and down Silverbell Road for several miles, all that
land along the river bottom there.

I can remember visiting my grandparents' home as a child.
That home was very old-fashioned. It was built out of adobe
with high walls and little windows way up high because at that
time there were still Apache Indians rounding up here, and the
little windows were used as lookouts. The house had a *zahuán*—
a wide entrance with double doors. You would walk through the
zahuán into the inner court, and at each side of the zahuán there
was the kitchen and other rooms. As you approached the house
on Silverbell Road, it was all fenced, and there were pomegranate
trees on both sides of the drive. We loved the pomegranates—
that I'll never forget! It was so sad when they knocked that house
down. My father was born in that house.

There was a big open area, and then a block or so away from
the house there was a dam. It was definitely man-made. The dam
would fill up with water when it rained and the river overflowed.
I remember that once or twice the older kids were allowed to go
and swim in the pond made by the dam and Mamá Grande,

Eloisa and Cirilo León, paternal grandparents of Livia, ca. 1885.

Eloisa, used to worry a lot because she was afraid that the children might drown. There was a lot of water because in those days it rained a lot. In later years, the represo dried up—where did all the water go? My grandmother and grandfather celebrated their saints' days. My grandmother's saint's day was *el día de San Pedro y San Pablo,* June 29. My grandfather's saint's day, San Cirilo, is July 9. Those days were almost like Christmas to us. Our only regret was that they were so close together. Those were days that we would spend with grandparents—*todo el día de celebrar.* It was a big family gathering and as many as could would come. They had three sons: Francisco, my father, and Antonio, who was well known for his business, Baffert and León. They had a daughter, Eloisa Ward, who lived in Willcox. My cousins were there. I remember the piñata. They'd play guitars and sing, and all the children would run around and play and get into scrapes. My grandmother always had goodies for us. She'd bake and cook. She made *biscochuelos* (anise cookies), *empanadas* (turnovers), and she baked her own bread. *Calabacitas con queso* (squash with cheese), *caldo de queso* (potato soup with cheese), *casuela* (beef jerky soup)—those were her specialties and they were good! She'd make us *machaca* (dried beef), and she dried the meat herself.

My mother's family had a very different history. My mother's name was Antonia Galáz. When she was born, her mother died, and my Great-grandmother Añastasia Coronado—we called her La Nana Tacha—raised her. She also helped to raise us many years later. That was the only mother my mother ever knew. My great-grandmother was from the area of Sahuripa, Sonora, and she was married to Francisco Coronado, who was a farmer. When Francisco died—he was already elderly—my mother was about eleven or twelve. They had very little. My great-grandmother was able to make a living because she was a *partera* (midwife). She took care of women in childbirth, and they paid her with *frijol* and *maiz*. She had a *comadre* (godmother) who kept writing and telling her to come to Tucson, that there was no future for her there in Mexico. So finally she did, about 1900, when my mother was thirteen years old. Even at that young age, my mother got a job as a babysitter for the Drachman family—Moses Drachman. She helped to raise Oliver and Rosemary Drachman. My mother was also very good with the needle, and she made clothes for the children. Mrs. Drachman—she was a very conscientious woman—realized my mother's potential and thought that she should be doing something besides babysitting. Mrs. Drachman had a friend by the name of Mrs. Cordis, who had a dressmaking shop where the old Levy's used to be on Pennington and Scott. Mrs. Cordis employed several girls to make beautiful clothes—even gowns—for the well-to-do women in Tucson. Mrs. Drachman got my mother a job there. She was sixteen when she became a seamstress, and that's how she supported herself and helped take care of my great-grandmother.

The barrio my mother and great-grandmother lived in was on

Antonia Galáz, Livia's mother, worked as a seamstress for ten years before she married. She made the dress and hat she is wearing in this 1905 photograph.

North 5th Avenue; it was still a very Mexican barrio at the time. My great-grandmother continued to practice her midwifery. "¿Doña Añastasia, me vas a atender?" "Pues sí, si me llames." ("Doña Añastasia, will you attend me?" "Of course, if you call me.") She was busy because the Mexican women had large families. My mother and great-grandmother were completely independent; they had their own little apartment on North 5th Avenue. My mother worked as a seamstress for ten years, until the time she got married. She made all her own patterns and taught herself by cutting and sewing. After she got married and had a family, she sewed for us all the time, including our wedding dresses and the wedding dresses of some of her granddaughters.

It was in that barrio that my mother first met the León family. She knew Francisco León first, and then she met my father. My parents were married in 1911, and they had nine children. Two died when they were little and so they raised seven of us: Solano, myself, Louis, Melania, the twins—Ermela and Eloisa—and Manuel. We were all born in Rillito, and my great-grandmother attended my mother at all our births.

When they were married, my father homesteaded at Rillito—

he was given 360 acres over there. Forty of it was supposed to be for farmland, and the rest for grazing. There were good years at the beginning; there was plenty of water. My father bought water that came through the *acequias*—he was entitled to so much. Then Cortaro Farms bought out all that area and came in with their huge pumps and depleted our water supply. We were located just east of them, east of the railroad tracks. The ditches began to dry up and with time *se emparejaron* (were leveled and filled with dust). I was about twelve, and I remember asking my mother, "¿Por qué no vamos a tener maiz este año?" "Porque no hay agua," me decía. ("Why aren't we going to have corn this year?" "Because there is no water," she'd answer.)

My father had a lot of trouble with water—those were also drought years—and the last few years of his life were very hard. In 1941, a year before he died, my mother just refused to continue to live with that and she said, "It's just too much. We are going to move into town. There must be something else we can do for a living." So he got rid of all the stock, but he would not sell the land. When he died, my husband became her administrator, and she kept after him: "Fermín, vende ese rancho; vende ese rancho." ("Fermín, sell the ranch.")

A big company bought it for a pittance. I remember in 1963 I told my husband, "Let's go out there and see. Maybe we can buy ten acres." We went out there, and he started investigating—it was in escrow with a big Eastern company that was holding it for speculation. They bought it for very little, and now you can imagine what it's worth. It's a huge development. It's right there at Rillito. Rillito was a railroad section house in those days. Now across the way is that Water Breakers Park. It doesn't seem possible that there was no water for our homestead and now that park is there and they have water galore.

It was a sad experience for me when I went out there, because it's so different now from what it was at one time, so modern with all those big places. And yet what I remember is our home there and the way it was sitting in the middle of the country. It was a nice big ranch home. It started out as a two-room adobe, and they kept adding on to it. My father always had two or three families to help him with our place; a ranch takes a lot of people to work it. If somebody wanted to work and take his family over there my father would say, "Yes, but you have to help build the place where you're going to live." All the men would get together and build a complete house in about two weeks, including the roof. They made the adobes, and my father supplied them with the rest of the materials. For a long time you could see these great big pits where they had made the adobes. I used to tell my father when I'd see those holes, "¡Ay, quisiera un swimming pool!" "¡Sí! A swimming pool!" There were about four little adobe houses around our ranch house. The families were very happy to be able to live out there. They'd put their children in school—the elementary school at Rillito was about a mile walking distance from our house.

We played with the children of the workers. My parents would allow us to invite them over; they were the only other children around. We played singing games. "Naranja Dulce" was one of them. We'd make a circle holding hands and sing:

Naranja dulce
Limón partido
Dame un abrazo
Que yo te pido

Si fueran falsos
Mis juramentos
En otros tiempos
Se olvidarán

Tocar la marcha
Mi pecho llora
Adiós Señora
Yo ya me voy

A mi casita de sololoi
A comer tacos
Y no te doy.

You'd be in the middle of the circle and choose the person you wanted the hug from; they'd come into the circle and you would go out, and it would be their turn to choose.

The other song and game was "Matarile rile rile."* We played it in two lines that came together. A person was chosen and went to the other line when he liked the title he was given (teacher, carpenter, etc.).

Agua y té,
Matarile rile rile
Agua y té
Matarile rile ron.

¿Qué quiere Ud.?
Matarile rile rile
¿Qué quiere Ud.?
Matarile rile ron.

Yo escojo a (name)
Matarile rile rile
Yo escojo a (name)
Matarile rile ron.

Le pondremos carpintero,
Matarile rile rile
Le pondremos carpintero
Matarile rile ron. (etc.)

We usually played on moonlit nights because we could see our shadows. I'm surprised I even remember. There are so many things that you don't think of for years and years and all of a sudden something triggers that thought, and it sends you back into that era. I remember saying, "¿Puedo ir a jugar con la Felícita?" "No. Ahora no. Hay, después, cuando termines tu trabajo."

---

*These games, called "rondas" in Spanish, are played in a circle or in lines with "nonsense" rhymes.

("Can I go play with Felícita?" "No, not right now. Later, when you have finished your work.")

We all had chores; everybody had something to do. Bring in wood. Bring water into the house. We had a well, and we had to fill the big barrels indoors with the water that was used for cooking and washing dishes and bathing. Later my parents got indoor plumbing, and my dad bought a Kohler Plant generator for electricity. But prior to that we used kerosene lamps. Washing was done outside on the washboard. You had to build a fire for hot water because in those days we boiled the clothes; that's why they were always so white. Later on, also, my dad bought my mother a Maytag, one that ran on gasoline.

One of my chores was to help with the ironing. I did it early in the morning before it got too hot. We ironed every morning for an hour or so. We'd put those little cast-iron irons on the stove to heat or on the coals outside. Mother had as many as six irons at once on the coals. They were *heavy*. Our clothes were all cotton, and everything was starched and ironed. There was no such thing as sending you to school with a wrinkled shirt or skirt! I still have one of those old *planchitas*; one time I went to the ranch before it was sold and I found it there. I also found a copper kettle of my mother's and a can of Prince Albert that had been my father's—he used to roll his own. Mother rented the place out there for a time, and a lot of things were taken. There is a lot of pilfering when things are left alone.

My brother Solano was my dad's shadow. He fenced. He went on roundups when they branded the cows. He also helped with the milking.

I helped my mother with all the household chores—cooking, cleaning, washing, ironing. But my sister Melania did not like housework, so she was allowed to do outside chores. She'd help my father and brother with the milking. After the cows were milked, the stalls had to be cleaned and washed, and that was one of her chores.

My mother and father both used to work very, very hard on that ranch. In the beginning my father just had the western cattle—the longhorn—but later on he got the jerseys so that we could have milk. Once we had the dairy cows, there was all that milk to be processed every single day to make cheese and butter. The people from the section house came and bought the cheese and butter. It was a little business in itself. My mother did that, and I helped her. We used tubs of milk to make cheese. We used rennet tablets to curdle the milk and then put the curdled milk into a press and gradually tightened it so that the whey separated from the cheese. Then it was put into a mold—they had big and small molds to make large and small cheese. My dad sold some of the cheese to the stores in town—*las tienditas* that they had in those days. They also used to make *quesadillas*—I don't mean a tortilla with a piece of cheese in it. The quesadillas were a special order, and there was much more work to them. The milk would curdle and settle to the bottom; then there was an aging process— it is like a cottage cheese that has been dried up very well. Then it was strained through a cheese cloth and cooked. My mother had a lot of friends who said to her, "Ay, Tonya, traígame una docena de quesadillas." ("Tonya, bring me a dozen quesadillas.") I don't remember what they sold them for, probably a song. You can still buy them over in Nogales, and they are very expensive.

My mother made a lot of baby clothes. People sought her out for a godmother for baptisms because she made such beautiful christening gowns that she gave to her *ahijados* (godchildren). She'd use the tiny little buttons for the baptismal gowns. She was an expert at making pintucks. They can be made by machine, but she made them by hand because they came out straighter. She made the garments out of very fine cotton batiste. She cut out the material big—¡*ay que grande lo estas cortando!* Because by the time she gathered in all those little pintucks in the bodice, the gown would be just right. She made all the little undergarments, too. All the little lace was hand applied. It was a pastime for her. At night she would sit and do all that fine handwork.

My mother was quite an artist with her sewing. She made us dolls out of cotton lisle stockings—*medias de hile*. Cotton stockings were very common in those days. Of course, silk stockings have always been on the market, but they were out of reach for people like us. If you had a pair of silk stockings you got them when you were a teenager and you had one pair, just for best. Las medias de hile were very pliable. Mother made the head, the body, the arms, and the legs, stuffed them with cotton, and then she joined all the parts together. She embroidered their faces, their eyes and mouths, and even their fingers. She made their braids out of yarn. Then she dressed them beautifully—they were *bien vestidas*! She made pretty little clothes out of scrap material—underwear, slips, dresses, pinafores, and little black shoes. She'd line shoeboxes and put them under the Christmas tree. It was such a surprise and a joy! Melania and I liked them very much, and we took good care of them. I wish I still had one! I tried to make one once, but I don't have the talent my mother had. *Me salieron las caritas muy feas.* (The little faces came out very ugly.)

And, oh yes! I remember our Christmas tree! Christmas trees were just becoming popular. There was no way that we could get a Christmas tree from town. My dad didn't believe very much in those things. But there was a tree in the *campo* (country) called a salt cedar. Solano went out and cut one and trimmed it so it would have the shape of a Christmas tree! We were delighted. Then, to show you how we made do, he cut the *tunas* (fruit buds) from the *viznaga* (barrel cactus) and chollas. We wrapped them in foil and hung them for decorations. We strung popcorn and pretty red cranberries. Mother made the star out of lace and shiny paper and put it on the top of the tree. And we had a pretty little tree out of everything that was there.

Cactus candy from the viznaga was one of our delicacies, too. My dad knew which viznaga made the best candy. It's just like any kind of fruit; it has to be tender and at its peak. Every year my dad and Solano would go to the desert and bring a viznaga home, and mother would process it. It required a lot of sugar and boiling. It had to be skinned and all the spines removed, and the pulpy center cut into chunks and soaked in a light solution of brine until firm. Then it was washed real well and put in a *tina grande* to boil on a fire outside. It was boiled with the sugar until it crystallized. There was processing from one tina to another. Aside from being a lot of work, it was a lot of fun. We'd all be there watching and trying to help and probably getting in the way! Mother would pack the candy in boxes and store it, and we'd have it during the year.

Mother didn't make the cactus candy only for us. She gave it to her friends and family for Christmas. There was a candy store on Congress Street in Tucson, called the Palace of Sweets, owned by a Greek family. They'd fix up the boxes with cactus candy cut in tiny little squares, and it sold for a good price. Mother had seen it there, and so she'd do the same thing.

In my youth there were a lot of simple things that brought us much pleasure and entertainment. A wonderful memory is the day we went with my dad to get *tortugas* (desert tortoises). There was a canyon about eight miles from the ranch called Cañon del Burro. There were a lot of caves there, and when it rained during the summer, the tortugas came out of their caves. Sometimes we found one or two and other times quite a few. Oh, how I remember when we went out for the tortugas! Mother gave us a lunch and we'd have a picnic; we'd go out and run free in the desert. I would like to return there someday, because I remember the wash with a lot of sand in that canyon.

My father liked turtle soup very much. The tortugas do not have much edible meat; just the *patitas* (legs) are good for eating. The patitas were cut off and cooked with bones and all, like neck bones. They boiled them until the thick skin and nails loosened. Then they peeled off the hide—nails and all—and the meat remained. Mother cooked the meat with onion, green chile, and tomato, and made a caldo that was like casuela. Very little meat but with a lot of substance and flavor.

My father saved turtle shells and cleaned and varnished them. Out of those shells my mother made tortoise-shell boxes for Christmas presents. She lined the shells with cotton covered with satin or silk. My father used a very fine file or an icepick and made holes in the shells and then put little tiny hinges on the breastplate. That was the lid. My mother and father spent a lot of time entertaining themselves like this. Little ones were used for jewel cases. The little larger ones were handkerchief boxes, and the ones made from large tortugas were sewing baskets. In the middle of the ones that were sewing baskets, Mother put little sticks for the spools of thread!

There was a teacher that I liked very much, and I wanted Mother to make a tortoise-shell box for her. The teacher was enchanted with it! My mother had given one to a friend—a *pariente*—and this woman was already quite elderly. Denise and I went to visit her, and Denise fell in love with it. She told Denise, "I'm going to give it to you because your grandmother made it for me and I want you to have it." That's the only one that I know of that exists.

We also enjoyed gathering saguaro fruit in the middle of June when the fruit turns bright red on top of the tall saguaro. My great-grandmother would not let one year go by without being taken two or three times to pick saguaro fruit. We had to get up real early in the morning before the sun came up, because it's very hot out there in the desert. When Nana Tacha was still alive, we had a *carretela* (buggy). Solano drove, and Melania and I went with them. Nana Tacha liked to sit there, and as we brought them down she'd have them for breakfast!

Solano made a saguaro pole as long as he could. It had a hook and with that he pulled down the ripe fruit at the top. Those were the real good ones. Some of them were already open, and those were as sweet as can be! Some were closed, but very pink. We had a big pan, and we'd gather them and bring them home. We'd let them sit for a few days and then open them up with a knife. It's a very sweet fruit; it has a lot of little tiny black seeds, but the meat is just delicious. Now the saguaros have acquired a certain disease. They don't bear the fruit the way they used to.

We also used the mesquite bean. The young mesquite tree bears beautiful beans, long and sweet. We chewed the seeds—*péchita* we called it. Nana Tacha boiled them and made *atole de péchita* (mesquite bean gruel). She used the whole bean. She washed it real well, boiled it, mashed it, ground it, and then sieved it to get the juice. She thickened the juice and sweetened it with *panocha* or *piloncillo* (brown sugar). It made a delightful pudding. We'd save it and we could eat it any time. My great-

Antonia and Luis León, Livia's parents, with Louis Ward, a nephew,
standing, *and children,* Livia, center standing, *Melania, and Solano, ca.*
1917.

grandmother taught us a lot of things for survival, making do
with what we had at hand. There was no waste in those days.

Solano and I learned to make tamales with my great-
grandmother. I remember that she would get a craving for tamales in the middle of the summer. And she would say, "Mihi-
jitos, vamos a hacer tamales." ("Children, we are going to make
tamales.") At one time, we harvested the dried corn and husked
it. My father had big machines that separated the cob from the
kernels. Then we soaked the corn in lime, and they ground it in
the grinding machine.

My mother and great-grandmother even made something out
of the whey that is left after you make the cheese and quesadillas.
It is called *requesón* and is like ricotta cheese. They put the whey
in a tub and built a fire under the tub and boiled the whey until
the foam came to the top. They spooned off the foam until they
filled a whole tub. My mother had three or four #3 tubs just for
the processing of the milk. The foam was stored, so it wouldn't

spoil like regular cheese because it had already been through the boiling process to kill the bacteria. You can spread it on tortillas or you can use it like butter.

Nana Tacha also used to fix *chicos*. They are a special kind of corn, a *maiz* with small kernels. She put the chicos right in the oven and toasted them while the kernels were still on the cob. They turned brownish and lasted indefinitely. Then she *los desgranaba* (shucked the kernels), let them soak overnight, and washed them real well the next day. They had to be cooked for a few hours, until they were tender. Then she added the red chile. At one time my dad had a little patch because Nana Tacha liked to make them. Not too long ago I was up in Northern Arizona. It was in the fall and the Indians had just harvested their chicos. In fact I bought some chicos from an Indian lady. She said, "I don't want to sell." I said, "Oh, but won't you sell me just a few?" "Well, all right. Five dollars." And that was high for just a few chicos, but I bought them because I had not seen them since my Nana Tacha fixed them.

My mother had a garden in those early years. She had vegetables and fruit trees, and I remember her telling us, "No se comen los duraznos mientras que están verdes—se van a enfermar." ("Don't eat the peaches while they are green or you will get sick.") She had a vineyard, and at one time she had so many grapes that she made wine. Nana Tacha dried the fruits and vegetables. She roasted and peeled tomatoes and green chile and dried them and put them in bags and stored them. We had no refrigerators, so everything had to be dried.

When my father butchered, we had fresh meat, but we also had a supply of *carne seca* (dried meat). It was a big job. They cut the meat into strips and put it into a box with screens to keep the flies out. My mother had to turn it repeatedly. It took days and days to dry the meat. They packed it in big muslin bags, and we had one or two of those for the year.

When my father butchered, he sold a lot of fresh meat to the people from the section house. It was a big heyday. Nothing was wasted; they would even buy *las pepenas*—the leavings—the heart, the liver, the tripe, and other organs. Everything was used, even the head. The horns were removed and cleaned very well and roasted whole in an oven. This was called "la tatema." The brains, cheeks, and tongue would be eaten. It is still considered quite a delicacy among ranchers.

My father dried the hides of the cattle and sold the rawhide in town. They were not affluent times, but we never lacked for anything. We were poor, but we felt rich. We had so much that we didn't feel we needed money wealth, that dollar.

When we became teenagers and interested in boys and girls, we had dances and a lot of parties. When I met Fermín in 1933, he started coming out to the ranch with some of his friends. My brothers had girlfriends who came out also. My mother's family was musically inclined. Her father had his own orchestra and my mother played the guitar, so I guess my brothers got that from her. Solano played the violin, Louis played the piano and guitar (he still has an orchestra), and my youngest brother, Manuel, played the violin. There was an *Americanito*, a friend of theirs from school, who used to come and play and that made the foursome. His name was Don Jones. He was so cute. He liked to sing in Spanish, but he didn't speak a single word of it!

At one time my dad had had a little store right there at the front of the house. It was a big room with a cement floor. He had it for about four or five years while there were people out there working on the railroad. He sold meat and cheese and stocked it with staples from town.

After he closed the store, he cleared out the room and it made a nice big dance floor, and that's where we had our parties. My mother played the guitar and my dad sang. There was a beautiful song they sang together, a duet:

LA ROSA

Yo vi una fresca rosa
Una mañana
Perfumada y graciosa

Tierna y lozana
Que bella estaba, que bella estaba.
Sobre su verde tallo
Se balanciaba, se balanciaba.

Al declinar la tarde
La vi ya muerta
Triste y silenciosa
Pálida y yerta.
Vino la brisa, vino la brisa
Y sus hojas se esparcieron
Como ceniza, como ceniza.

Así pasan en el mundo
Las ilusiones, los placeres
Y las pasiones
Y de este modo, y de este modo
En esta triste vida
Todo se acaba, se acaba todo.

THE ROSE

I saw a fresh rose
One morning,
Perfumed and beautiful
Tender and verdant
How beautiful it was, how beautiful it was.
It swayed, it swayed,
On its green stem.

As the sun declined,
I saw that it was dead
Sad and silent
Pale and motionless.
The breeze blew, the breeze blew
And its leaves scattered
Like ashes, like ashes.

That is how illusions and pleasure
And passions pass in the world.
In this manner, in this manner
Everything is finished,
Everything ends.

I looked up to my father—he was my mentor. He did not have a formal education, but he had a beautiful command of Spanish and English. He spoke a very flowery Spanish. He read to us in Spanish, and to this day I feel that my Spanish and English are good because of him. He did not want us to speak English with an accent. He did not tolerate slang; we were immediately corrected. If we had to learn a poem in school—we had a teacher who believed a lot in memorizing and recitation—he would sit there and memorize the poem with us. I still have some of my father's old books. Where he acquired them I don't know. Some of them have copyrights that go back to the 1800s. He had Shakespeare; he had Chaucer, Cervantes, Victor Hugo, and Alejandro Dumas.

My parents were very, very religious—my father through books and a Bible and my mother, as a cradle Catholic. My father taught us all the religion he knew; he read us the Bible. We had morning prayers and the rosary every single night.

When my husband-to-be first started coming to visit, it was a real education for him to be told that it was rosary time, but before long he found himself saying the rosary right along with us. After we married, we had rosary time with our own children until they were in high school and college.

A cradle Catholic, that's what I call myself, because with my religion there is just no question; it's inbred in you. There is that Divine Power up there that guides your life every day that you get up. The ranch life is hard, and you learn to take adversity as well as the good times. I remember, when I was in my teens, getting impatient with my father because everything was "God's will." "Si Dios dirá; Si Dios lo manda." But when you get older you realize that there are some things you can control and some things you can't, and if you are patient and accepting, it's so much easier.

And, oh, *Diosito*, my mother was so old-fashioned! She was very strict and straitlaced. She did not believe in makeup. When we were in high school, we were not allowed to go on picnics or to dances. She felt that we had to be chaperoned, but at that time chaperones were already a thing of the past. When I met Fermín, the only reason that I was allowed to date was that I went out with my brother. Also, when they knew Fermín, they liked him so much that I had no problems, but she continued being strict with my sisters.

I went to grade school in Rillito and then I attended high school in Marana. I graduated in 1931 when I was sixteen. I wanted very much to go to the Teacher's College in Tempe. At that time you could work your way through. My mother would not allow it. "No! Andarte tú sola allá—no, no, no, no!" My father was a little more lenient, but she put her foot down. Those were the Depression years; things were real tight, and they did not have the money. Later on, when I was eighteen, they paid my way through commercial school for nine months—Cox Commercial School down on Stone Avenue. I took a course and worked there—clerking, stenography—and then I worked as a clerk at the Alianza Hispano Americana for about a year. While I was there, I met a man named Justo Chavez. He and his wife lived on Palomas Avenue. I was still living at the ranch and coming in every day with a cousin. It was really not very convenient, but my mother was not very happy about my being away from home so much. They offered me a room to rent. My mother had to meet them, and she approved, so I moved in with them for about a year. Later, when Mr. Chavez went to the legislature I worked as an attaché for two sessions in Phoenix.

I got married in 1935 to Fermín Montiel. His father, Ralph, had started a moving and storage company in 1926, but he died when he was only forty-two years old and left nine children in the family. Fermín was the oldest, and the baby, the only girl in the family, was only seven months old. I've already told you about my ranch life during the Depression years, but life in town was

Livia León Montiel with her husband, Fermín, and family on the occasion of their twenty-fifth wedding anniversary, ca. 1960.

much harder; it was a daily thing just to survive. Fermín did not have a youth; he took over the responsibility of his mother and all those children. His father left him with just one truck and it was not paid for, but Fermín was an ambitious man and got the truck paid off. It was just hand-to-mouth providing for his family.

By the time we got married in 1935, he had a little office across from the Southern Pacific Depot, just room enough for a little desk and a telephone. He needed someone very badly to answer the phone because he had two trucks—a driver and a helper on one and he was the driver on the other. So that's where I came in. The first year of my marriage was spent in that little office answering the phone, taking orders, helping as much as I could. In 1936 we needed another place, and there was a service station for rent across from the Governor's Corner on Court Street, and we rented that. It had two or three rooms, and we figured that we could have the office and live there. I was working in the office and helping in the family business and still was able to be at home. Of course, I was having children right along—eight children. Later, when things were going well, he hired someone to help in the office. The war years were good years, and those were the years he was expanding—buying trucks, getting into that huge warehouse out on the freeway. I had always helped out when he needed extra office help, but after 1950 I worked in the office quite a bit, and my mother and my sister Ermela helped me with the children. My mother was a big influence in my children's life. She had a good relationship with them, especially with Chickie (Marie), my oldest daughter. By that time, of course, she had become more liberal, more lenient about modern ways.

Business was good and we prospered, except later competition got very bad and Fermín was not well. He lived under a lot of stress and got ulcers. In 1972 he had his coronary. By that time he had to be away a lot and business went down. He sold the business in 1973 just to get out, but he was very conscientious and paid all his debts. He died on May 20, 1981.

As we get older, what we live with is our memories that we have treasured away. That's the only thing we have left in the end. I think of my youth and my grandparents and my parents. I think of the gatherings that meant so much to us. We really looked forward to them; they were so important in our life that we kept thinking, "It's like Christmas." And I want to hold the family together and leave this legacy for my children and for my grandchildren. If my grandchildren can remember, "Well, when we went to Grandma's house it was this way and that way and we had such a good time."

This is how I began my reunions: It was supposed to be a celebration of Chickie's twenty-fifth anniversary, but it didn't work out that way. Fermín had died, and there was a funeral instead. So the next year, on the first anniversary of Fermín's death, I went to Benson and talked to Fr. Rossetti. I asked him if he would come and say a mass for Fermín, and he said yes. So the next year I wrote to Chickie and told her to come—we were going to have a twenty-fifth plus one anniversary. It was a memorial mass and an anniversary. I invited the whole family on both sides, and that night, when I was getting ready to say good-bye, I said that I was going to make this an annual affair. They all loved it. The second and third year I started with the grandchildren's talent show, and I built a ramada and little stage just for that. The grandchildren dance and sing; they recite and play the piano; they dance *folklórico*. Now we are going into the ninth year.

Fr. Carrillo has said the mass; Fr. Burns; Fr. Rossetti. The priests all liked Fermín very much. He did a lot for the Church. And I got a mariachi one year, and now they want a mariachi every year. It is very beautiful. I call this reunion "the Memorial," and all my family looks forward to it. It is a two-day affair. On Saturday we have the mass and *barbacoa*, and on Sunday a brunch.

I am very happy with what I have today. I'm glad the Lord has given me enough life to see it this way. When I have these reunions, I have all my and Fermín's brothers and sisters. The only way you can hold your family together is by uniting with them from time to time. Today everybody lives in a different place—we are all so scattered. It isn't like people used to live in the same barrios for years and years, so it is necessary to have these reunions as often as possible. I'd like to leave this piece of land just as a gathering place for all of them. I don't know what they'll do when I'm gone, but I have told the girls how I feel, and I think that they will try to keep it going. Land is becoming extinct, and all this will be developed. If it would only be possible for them to hold on to this little piece of land for all of them to reunite from time to time. This is my hope and my legacy. *Pero no me quiero morir poniendo voluntades.* (But I don't want to die making demands.)

Julia Yslas Vélez

MY NAME IS JULIA YSLAS VÉLEZ. I was born in 1910 in San Miguel de Horcasitas, Sonora, Mexico. At one time San Miguel was the capital of the state of Sonora, and I believe that some of the governors from Spain lived there, had a palace there. My mother's name was Josefa Sasturaín de Yslas; her father was from Spain, and he opened a soap factory in town. He was very elderly, and when he died my grandmother came to live with us. She always lived with us—she raised us. She was wonderful to us. Her name was Marcela Tapia Sasturaín. Tapia was a prominent name in Horcasitas and I think somewhere along the line she was related to Alvaro Obregón, the president of Mexico. My grandmother was very stately, very thin, very aristocratic looking. She had long hair, and they called her La Chinita because her hair was curly. She was very beautiful.

I remember when my grandmother and I used to visit her brother. He had the biggest store in San Miguel de Horcasitas. He ordered merchandise from Europe, and he also sold beautiful material. In fact, he was called "El Tirita" because people would buy cloth by the yard—*metros*—and they would say, "Why don't you give us a pilón—otra tirita." And so he would give them a little strip of extra material. He was very rich, and I remember he had a roomful of gold coins, but I don't think he helped my grandmother out very much.

My father's name was Antonio Yslas Urías. I think my father was born in Ures, Sonora. My father and mother had nine children, but three died and so they raised six of us. My father had a ranch on the outskirts of Horcasitas, and our house was in town. It was beautiful property because the river divided the land. I do not want you to get me wrong. When my mother and father lived in Mexico with the six of us, we were not poor. My father had cattle. He would butcher one cow a week, and he would feed all of us and give the rest away to the neighbors. Of course, we had a farm; we had all the vegetables we wanted to eat. And he had dairy cows. My mother would get up at three in the morning to milk the cows and make cheese—*requesón, cuajada*. And my dad had beautiful horses. I remember when my two handsome

The Yslas family in San Miguel de Horcasitas, Sonora, Mexico, ca. 1900. From left to right: Marcela Tapia Sasturaín, grandmother holding María; Josefa Sasturaín de Yslas; mother of Julia; Antonio Yslas Urías, Julia's father; and brother Augustín. In front are Francisco and Fernando. Arizona Historical Society Library: Mexican Heritage Project.

brothers, Fernando and Pancho, used to come in from the ranch, the girls would stand up on the walls to watch them come into town on their beautiful horses. My father was very handsome also; he was very fair and had a big moustache.

As I said, we were not poor, but it was a simple life. My mother used to grind all her wheat in a *metate*; my sisters would help her, but I was too small. All I did was play and roam around the neighborhood. I remember one winter morning when I was very small, I had on a nice winter coat and my mother was watching me. Along came a donkey and he made a funny noise and it scared me. Instead of running back to the house, I ran and fell into a well. Some of my mother's calves had fallen in that well and died instantly on the rocks at the bottom. But I fell on the side into the water. The president of the town heard my mother's screams, and he went into the well and got me out. I don't know how he made it; he was a very fat man with a big stomach. I guess God wanted to save me for something. We used to sleep on mattresses made of grass, what they call *petates*. We didn't have much furniture, just a table and some benches. We didn't have any washing machines or gas stoves. We used to cook on an *estrado* with a wood fire. It's like a barbecue pit, built up with high sides made out of adobe; then a metal sheet was put on top, and that's where you put your pots. At one time, many years later, when I was a young woman of about twenty, I went to visit my father in Horcasitas, and he told me to put some beans on. I cleaned the beans and put some water and beans in the pot and put it on the estrado to cook. But I let it go, and the bottom of the pot came off. I wasn't used to it. Sometimes my mother would even make her own dishes. She would use some of the fine clay from the river for her dishes.

In those days we didn't know anything about Christmas. Our toys were the wee little bones from the cows. We'd build houses with little bones. That's why, to this day, when I eat *menudo* and I get a *huesito*, I always love it, and I say to myself, "This was my toy when I was a child." We used to play with dirt and make clay and make little dishes. The only thing that I remember about Christmas is when I was about three or four years old. My sisters took me to the different houses and we knocked on the doors and sang:

En Belén nació Jesús
Por ser hijo de María
Los reyes
Y los señores
Dan aginaldo este día.

Christ was born in Bethlehem
Because he was the son of Mary
Kings and gentlemen
Give offerings on this day.

They would give me candy, but we never had any Christmas presents.

We came to the United States because the Yaqui Indians were very fierce and did not like my father; they were killing people everywhere. My two brothers and their *peón* were working on the farm near San Miguel. The Indians captured them, and they were taken prisoner. After a while the Yaquis killed the little Indian peón with rocks, but the Indians told my brothers that they did not want to kill them; they wanted to use them as interpreters. So as they were walking along the river, they made my brothers step on the stones so they would not leave a trail. I'm not sure how my dad heard about it, but he went into town and gathered some men on horseback. They were armed. My father found them at dusk. The Indians had built a big fire. My dad said to his men, "Don't fire until I fire the first time." He fired, and the Indians got scared and ran away, and both of my brothers ran to my father.

I was six years old when we left San Miguel de Horcasitas. We left the house and everything. We came to Nogales because my dad had a brother there. When my father was about seventeen or eighteen, he worked as a forest ranger in Yuma, so he already knew English. He must have already had a job, because we went straight to Aguirre's ranch near Sasco. He did ranch work; he was a *vaquero*, but we only lived there for a short time. Then we moved to Sasco, near Silverbell, Arizona. My father and my brothers were blacksmiths in Sasco. There was a blacksmith shop there because of all the ranches and mines. It was a thriving town. There was even a theater, and Mr. Lim Goon had a grocery store there—*muy surtido* (lots of merchandise). My sister got a job in his store. She must have been around seventeen. About ten years ago I went back to Sasco with my family, and there isn't anything left there anymore, just the ruins.

I had my first schooling in Sasco. It was a one-room schoolhouse and the teacher was Anglo. Since I didn't speak any English, I didn't learn too much. I remember that we used to do a lot of singing; we sang "America the Beautiful." What I remem-

Julia Yslas at age six, Sasco, Arizona. Arizona Historical Society Library: Mexican Heritage Project.

ber especially was Christmastime, the big Christmas trees and snowmen and the stockings with candy and fruit and toys. That was all new to me. When we moved to Tucson I entered the first grade again. I didn't graduate from high school until I was nineteen. I lost a lot of time as a child.

We moved from Sasco to Tucson because my father and my brothers got better jobs. My brothers worked in the blacksmith shop for the county—an old building that still stands on Park and 2nd Avenue—and my father worked at La Piedriera, the rock quarry on "A" Mountain. We lived at first on the corner of Meyer and McCormick; from Meyer Street we moved to Kennedy where my grandmother died. From Kennedy we moved to 17th and then to Main Street and McCormick where we rented one of the houses that belonged to Mr. Otero.

My father eventually went back to Mexico and sold his cattle, and with the money he built us a house on South 4th Avenue between 20th and 21st. The house is still standing, and that is where we lived until even after I was married, until my mother died.

I went to Drachman School and then to Safford, and then I graduated from Tucson High. When I was in Drachman, I was voted the most popular girl in school. I was Miss Liberty in the Armistice Parade, and while I was at Safford, I played the part of Queen Elizabeth in a play. But you see, my father was not happy here. He eventually went back to Horcasitas to live, and so my mother depended on me. When I was in high school, I started working to help my mother out. I worked at Kresses for $1.65 a day. I used to give my mother $.50; I kept $.50 for my lunches at school during the week, and paid for my piano lessons. I couldn't be in athletics at Tucson High because I went to work after school. In the summer I worked all day at Kresses in all the departments.

To make a little more money, my mother started to sew. She had a little treadle machine, and she was self-taught and self-employed. At that time there were poor families living in railroad cars on South Park, and she sewed for them. She made everything—little shirts and dresses. I used to drive a little car and take her and her goods to sell to the families. She did not have a formal education, but she was very smart. She had a little book—I wish that I had kept it after she died. She used to mark in it what people owed her. She would draw a circle for a dollar and a half circle for fifty cents. She was very *luchona*; she struggled a lot, and she saved her money. She had money in the bank when she died.

I remember a time in Mexico when the money being circulated wasn't worth anything. It was called *bilimbiquis*. My father had done some kind of job and been paid with bilimbiquis, so she took the sack of money and went to the Governor's Palace and told them that her husband was sick, had been paid with worthless money, and she needed to have it exchanged for good money. They sent her from office to office, but she didn't give up, and finally she arrived at the office of the man in charge. They replaced the bilimbiquis. There were long lines of people waiting with their sacks of worthless bills. My mother was very happy; from there we went to a store, and I remember seeing a beautiful doll that I wanted very much, but she wouldn't buy it for me; I don't know why.

Even though I always had to work, I never forgot about finishing school. One of my brothers would tell my mother: "Why is she still going to school? She is too old; she is already eighteen!" And I used to hear that and get scared and think to myself: "No. I *am* going to finish school." I was trying to get an education so that I could get an office job. I took shorthand; I took typing and bookkeeping; I was a star student in algebra. I thought of going to the university many, many times, but my mother needed me; I had to support her.

The day I graduated from high school I got a job as a stenographer in the office at Albert Steinfeld and Company. I stayed at Steinfelds for about three years. The Depression came and since I was the youngest member of the office force, I was let go. Then I got a job at Lyric Outfitters—it was a credit store on the corner of Meyer and Congress. I had to keep all the accounts and my bookkeeping came in handy there. After that I worked for another credit store—Federal Clothing Store. For a while I didn't have a job and so I decided to go to Tijuana with my mother to visit my sister. While I was there I got a job in a curio store; I was in charge of the perfume department. It was owned by a very rich man by the name of Don Miguel Gonzáles. He was so rich that he was called El Mono de Oro.

While I was in Tijuana I met my husband, Emilio Vélez. He was from Magdalena and was working there as a mechanic. I had worked all those years, and I finally met the right man, but my mother still didn't want me to get married—even at twenty-nine! She thought I was still too young. We were married in 1939, and I went to live in Magdalena for a short time. But I worried about my mother; I felt that I had to come back and take care of her. So I emigrated with my husband, and we moved back to Tucson and lived with my mother in her house until she died.

Emilio Vélez and Julia Yslas Vélez in 1939. Arizona Historical
Society Library: Mexican Heritage Project.

My husband used to work for Bogard GMC Trucking Company as a mechanic, and we lived in a two-room house on Avia-
tion Drive. Then we bought a lot in South Tucson on West 34th
and 7th, just a block west of 6th Avenue. We built a house there
a little at a time; we kept adding. It was just a little house with no
windows or doors and an outside latrine. But we ended up with
a very nice eight-room house. I had a beautiful Virgen de Guadalupe in tile over the mantel. My husband also built a garage
there; he was a master mechanic, self-taught, and I guess you
could say it was in his blood. He could just listen to a car running
and he would know what was the matter with it. He used to em-
ploy little kids to sweep and wash the tools, and I used to tell my
husband: "Why don't you teach your own children?" But he told

Julia, right, Magdalena, Sonora, with sister-in-law Amparo Vélez, children Josie and Manny, and niece Lupe Félix in the late 1940s. Arizona Historical Society Library: Mexican Heritage Project.

me, "If they want to learn mechanics, let them learn at the university." We did well for a time, but there were hard times, too. I worked to make ends meet. I sold medicine house-to-house— Raleigh products. I put on Stanley parties; I demonstrated home products not only in Tucson, but also in Ajo and even in Magdalena and Hermosillo.

My husband died when he was only forty-six years old. He had a heart attack and was in a coma for thirteen days. So I was left with a big bill from the hospital. I paid every cent of it. I had to rent part of my house. I lived in two back rooms with my four kids. I stayed up until three o'clock in the morning making paper wreaths to sell for El Día de Los Muertos. I just couldn't make it with one job. I had two or three jobs. At one time I was working at the Salpointe Cafeteria. I wanted to work there because the boys were in school, and I wanted to be close to my kids. From there I would go home and fix dinner and then go to work for Lyric Outfitters, which had by this time moved to Southgate Shopping Center.

All my kids went to All Saints and then to Salpointe. I always made a sacrifice to send them to Catholic schools, because I was out in the field working and I couldn't teach them religion. Religion has always been very important to me. It has been like a brake when temptation came and like a guiding light during the hard times. After my boys finished Salpointe, I worked at the auto license department for eight-and-a-half years while they were in college.

I was fifty-five years old when I entered politics. I was on the South Tucson City Council for twelve years. I went into politics because I love people; I love crowds. And also because it might help my boys—you know—get better jobs. It paid $100 a month, and that helped my kids. I was the first woman on the South Tucson City Council. There had been another woman who had been the mayor, but that was a long time ago. We had a town manager, Paul Laos, who believed that we should go to all the conventions that we could, because it was a good education and we learned what the other cities were doing. I used to go to Washington and fight for my people. I would tell them that there were people here who didn't have running water, electric lights, or indoor plumbing. They were cooking indoors with wood stoves. While I was on the council, we bought a trailer park on South 6th Avenue where the new council offices are now. We built two homes for the elderly on East 29th Street—El Señorial and the Bernie Sedley Home. My name is on one of the plaques. We paved some of the streets and put in lights. I have always enjoyed helping the poor. When I worked in the cafeteria at Salpointe, there was always a lot of food left over, and I used to take it to the poor people in South Tucson. They loved me. In fact, there's a little old lady— she must be about one hundred years old—that I still visit. I take her money. When she sees me, she hugs me and cries with me.

It's like she has seen a miracle. I got off the council because I moved away from South Tucson. I sold the house and the garage. Now I live with my daughter. But when I lived on West 34th Street I would visit the neighbors; I used to sit outside on the porch and watch people pass by, like they do in the Mexican homes in Mexico. I miss that.

When my kids were small, there was an empty lot right in front of my house, and all the neighborhood kids played there— baseball and what not—but my kids didn't. My kids were helping me with the house before I left for work and before they left for school. That's why, when we were having our meetings and parks were being discussed and someone would say "We want parks for our kids!" I used to say, "We want jobs for our kids. We want education for our kids." I didn't believe in parks because my kids never played in parks; they were struggling right along with me.

I remember attending a meeting in Washington, D.C., while I was on the council. It was a black caucus. I loved the way this black lady spoke: "I want black faces in high places." So I took that for my motto. "I want Mexican faces in high places." This is the advice I gave my children: "I want you to make good in school, because I am the poorest in the family, and that is the inheritance I want to leave you—a good education." They believed it and followed it. My daughter Josie went back to school after she had raised her family; she has a very good job. She is secretary to the principal at Los Niños Elementary School. Manny has a master's degree and teaches English and writing at Pima College. Gilbert is director of a mariachi group and has a restaurant and karate school. Bill has a doctorate and is a tenured mathematics professor at the University of Arizona.

Of course, I don't have to work anymore, but I like to keep busy. I used to help Manny out at his real estate office. I work in the karate school office four afternoons a week. I would be at the restaurant every night if they would let me.

It was a hard life, but we made it.

CANCIÓN

Para Mi Madre, Julia   *Navidad de 1982*
The following verses, written by my son William,* were a Christmas gift
to me showing that a mother's labors are not in vain.

TU HERENCIA ES LO QUE NOS GUÍA LOS PASOS

Veía los charcos en la banqueta, como islas
En mi camino.
De pronto, no se por qué,
Me puse conciente del movimiento
De mis pies.

Seguros eran mis pasos.

Firme la tierra bajo mis pies.

Usted me ha facilitado el camino
Con su ternura y su trabajo
Aun siento sus esfuerzos respaldándome
Y ahora puedo decir:

Seguros son mis pasos.

Firme la tierra bajo mis pies.

¿Y qué de mis hijos?
Esta herencia pasará por mi
Sin perder el fervor que fue formado por Ud.
En los años que vienen
Su voz
A través de mí
Gritará con orgullo

Seguros son mis pasos

Firme la tierra bajo sus pies.

                    Su hijo,
                    Guillermo

SONG

For My Mother, Julia   *Christmas 1982*

YOUR INHERITANCE GUIDES OUR STEPS

I saw the puddles on the sidewalk
Like islands in my path.
Suddenly, I don't know why,
I became aware of the movement
Of my feet.

Confident were my footsteps

Solid the earth beneath my feet.

You have facilitated our way
With your tenderness and your labors.
Even now I feel your efforts supporting me
And I can say

Confident are my footsteps

Solid the earth beneath my feet.

And what of my children?
This inheritance shall pass through me
Without losing the fervor
Which you gave it.
And in the years to come
Your voice,
Through me,
Shall cry out with pride:

Confident shall be your footsteps

Solid the earth beneath your feet.

Your son,
William

*Used by permission of the author.

Paulina Moreno Montoya

MY NAME IS PAULINA MORENO MONTOYA. I was born in Redington, Arizona, on January 26, 1905. My mother's name was Vicente Soto de Moreno. Her father's name was Cayetano Soto; my mother came to the Tanque Verde area near Tucson from Mexico when she was nine years old. She told me that her father left Mexico because of a war.* They left in the middle of the night with only their clothes on their backs. My father's name was Trinidad Moreno; he was from Mexico, also, but by way of El Paso, Texas, where he worked with mules making watering holes for cattle. At least that's what my mother used to tell me, because I was only five years old when he died, and I do not remember him very well. There were eight children in our family: Manuel, Tomás, Antonio, Juana, Rita, Ramona, myself, and Elvira. Paula is my real name, but my sisters didn't like that name because it sounded like a boy's name, so they always called me Paulina.

My father was a farmer, and he also had cattle. He was a partner of Emilio Carrillo in Tucson, and he spent a lot of time there. My mother used to tell me that a lot of Tucson belonged to Emilio Carrillo—the old Tucson, that is. The Tanque Verde and other *ranchos* on the other side of El Rincón belonged to him also.

Redington is on the other side of El Tanque Verde—over the Rincon Mountains along the Río San Pedro. After my father died, my mother inherited his ranch and she leased it out. People would farm it. My brother had a ranch, and that is where we lived after my father died. I remember that my mother had dairy cows. She had twenty-four cows, and she milked the cows and made cheese—*queso y quesadillas*—and took them to the little store up there by the ranchos of the Vásquez family.

A few years after my father died, my mother married Jesús Ronquio. Cayetano Ronquio, who is my half-brother, still lives in Redington on my stepfather's ranch, but I don't believe that any of the *viejitos* (old-timers) are left there anymore. But I re-

*Editor's note: The chronology of the Sotos' flight suggests that the war mentioned is very likely the war against French occupation.

In the milpa at Redington, left to right, *Elvira and Paulina Moreno, Cayetano Ronquio, and Ramona Moreno, ca. 1920.*

member that there were a lot of farms and ranches along the river then—the Vásquez family, the family Tiznado, and farther up the river the Sosas, the Gámez, the Munguia. Those were some of the families that lived there.

I remember the farms in Redington—all vegetables. The people lived off the land; they planted oats, wheat, frijol, garbanzos, tepary beans, onions, chile verde, melon, because in those days they had to grow everything themselves. In the beginning there were no real stores there. It wasn't until much later—I think I was about thirteen years old—that they opened a store in the place called Cascabel. An Americanito came and opened a store and all *la Mexicanada* brought him the produce that they had harvested, and he gave them goods in trade. He had everything in that store—canned goods, clothes, cloth, shoes, candy. They called that area Cascabel (Rattle) because they killed a huge rattlesnake in that place. It was so large that they said that you could stretch the skin from one side of the road to the other. They had never seen a rattlesnake of that size before.

The provisions came from Tucson to the little store in Cascabel about once a month. Of course, there were no cars in those days, so I am talking about horse-drawn wagons. I remember as many as a dozen horses pulling those wagons. It would take eight days to make the round-trip from Tucson—four days to arrive and four days to return. There was a road through Oracle, and there were lots of ranchos along the way. The wagon stopped at all the ranchos. That old road doesn't exist anymore; the river took it all.

My mother told me that the river was narrow when they first came to Redington. They used just a little board to cross the river. My father had his fields there; everything was cultivated—even the sides of the hills—all the way from Benson to Winkleman. But the river got wider and wider, and it swept away my father's fields and the house we lived in. Can you imagine—they tell me that Winkleman is on the banks of the river now!

There were great mesquite forests along the Río San Pedro, and the houses were practically hidden in the *mesquital*. To me it was beautiful, but the teachers who came to Redington never stayed because they thought that it was too ugly and isolated. I went to school in Redington when there were teachers, but they often never lasted more than a month—just long enough to go back on the next supply wagon. All the teachers that went to Redington were Americanas, but I only spoke Spanish, since I never did learn English because I wasn't in school long enough. I lasted about three years in school; I guess I lost interest because school was so off and on.

How I loved to go horseback riding! My brother and I used to fight over a horse my mother had bought for me; it was a beautiful little horse—small and very fat. We called it "Pretty Baby." My brother would tell me, "I am going to mount him, and I am going to spur him and make him rear, so you'd better not try to ride him." But he never reared with me. On Sundays and on fiesta days a bunch of us kids would go horseback riding; we rode all along the river and up the hills to the mountains, all over the sierra.

I had a very good friend named Rita Vásquez. Her father was

a farmer and a rancher, but he was also a musician. Rita also played the guitar. My mother used to say that before my time Mr. Vásquez and his three brothers, who were also musicians, put on very lovely dances. Later on, Rita's father was the only one of the brothers who still played; he played the violin, but if there was someone else who played the violin, then he would play the flute. Joaquin Vásquez, one of the brothers, built a big dance hall in Redington where we danced. There were some very big fiestas. We danced till dawn. We danced waltzes, the mazurka, polkas, the two-step, and the *varsoviana*. When the sun came up, we'd still be dancing! People came from everywhere for the dances—from up the river, from all the little ranchos in the mountains. Even the Americanos—the Tejanos—who used to have ranchos around there danced with us. They mixed with the Mexicanada because that's all there was. But I didn't like to dance with them. They were not very good dancers. My mother chaperoned us, but after my sister Juana and brother Tomás died, she was sad and didn't want to go to the dances anymore. My sister and her husband Pedro and my brother died of the influenza in Mexico. They had gone there because they had heard rumors of the war. We lived in isolation, and people did not really know what was going on, so they got scared when they heard about the war and fled to Mexico. After my brother and sister died, one of the brothers of my Stepfather Ronquio chaperoned us.

The special fiesta days were September 16 (Mexican Independence Day), El Día de San Juan (June 24), El Día de San Pedro (June 29), and Christmas. On Christmas Eve we had a *velación* (vigil) for el Santo Niño, the Holy Child. We recited the rosary to el Santo Niño and sang *alabanzas* (praises). On Christmas we had a fiesta and dinner with enchiladas and tamales, and my stepfather brought us candy and oranges. We didn't have toys in those days, but we made our own dolls out of rags. Then all the *muchachería* (girls) would get together and play house along the banks of the river. We pretended to cook and eat like grown-up people, but only with our rag dolls.

People would get together and pray on holy days and saints' days. Of course, there was no church in Redington, but my mother used to tell me of a little chapel on the Sosa's ranch up the river, and the priest went there to say mass and hear confessions. We had catechism taught to us, I remember, by a very, very old lady. She was very strict. We had a different lesson every day. She read certain passages from the Bible, and we prayed in the morning and in the evening. "No rezar, no comer." ("If we didn't pray, we didn't eat.") But she was not as strict as the viejita who taught my children catechism when we lived in San Simón. There, if the children were late, she punished them by making them kneel on corn pebbles and hold heavy rocks with their arms uplifted.

A couple of my sisters didn't like Redington. They preferred city life. One of them moved to Willcox where we had family, and another moved to Tempe where she was married. I was the most *casera* (homebody) of all of them. I was about twelve or thirteen when I started to work in the *milpas* (fields) with my friend Rita Vásquez. Rita was a very hard worker and the only one who helped her father. We worked picking corn and chile, plowing, and planting. They paid however they could, and I used the money to help with necessities.

Before I got married my mother would send me up to La Bellota Ranch, high in El Rincón, to stay with my sister, Juana. That is where she lived when she got married to Pedro López, who was a vaquero. When we went up there, my brother-in-law had to blaze the trail.

When Pedro worked there, La Bellota belonged to Ben McKenzie, who lived in Tucson but went there to check on things. La Bellota was a ranch so high in the mountains that the only place you could look was up; the only thing you could see were the stars. At night we could hear the wolves howl. My mother sent me up there to stay with Juana because she was often left alone. I kept her company. We pretty much just stayed and tended to the house, but when it was *bellota* (acorn) season, we'd go and pick bellotas. When there were *corridos* (roundups), a lot of vaqueros gathered there. Although my sister shared the kitchen of the big ranch house, she did not cook for the cowboys. They had their own cook—an old black man.

I met my husband, Manuel Montoya, in Redington. He was

from the area of Dos Cabezas; his father, Quirino Montoya, was originally from Santa Fe, New Mexico. His mother, Dolores López Montoya, was, I believe, from the Cananea area. They had a boarding house for the miners at Mascot, a mining camp in the mountains above Dos Cabezas. My husband didn't stay there. He was a vaquero and came to Redington looking for work. We got married in Tucson on January 21, 1921, at the Tucsonia Hotel; in those days everyone came to Tucson to get married.

For a time, my husband Manuel worked in Redington, and then we moved to a lot of different places in the sierra. We had eight children, but our twins died. My first child was born at the Sierra Bonita Ranch with a midwife; the second, in Benson with a doctor; the third in Redington with no one. My mother was upset. She wanted me to go to Benson to have the baby, but I told her that I didn't want to go. If I was going to die, I wanted to stay in Redington.

The Sierra Bonita Ranch belonged to Colonel Hooker; it was near the little town of La Bonita. My husband worked there. He was a "jack of all trades"; there wasn't anything he couldn't do. He was a cook, a cowboy, a wrangler, a jockey. Because he was a small man, they used to call him "Chapo," "Shorty," and he rode in the horse races in the Tucson area. He was a very hard worker and all my children took after him. He was most famous for his fence building. He built miles and miles of *retaque* fences—the old-fashioned kind with mesquite branches—as well as the kind with posts and barbed wire.

We had a nice big house on the Hooker Ranch—four rooms. I did the washing and ironing for the Hooker family—everything by hand with a washboard, heating the water outside in a big kettle on a fire. Every single article that was worn or used in that house—as many as twenty sheets at a time—I washed and ironed. I washed and ironed for Mr. Hooker himself. All he wore were white shirts with those high, old-fashioned collars of *sololoi* (celluloid). *¡Un altero de ropa, Señora!* (A mountain of clothes!) I worked very hard. I used a cast iron which I heated on the wood stove, and I stood all day long.

From the Hooker Ranch we lived in La Bonita for a time; from

Manuel "El Chapo" Montoya,
husband of Paulina Moreno
Montoya, and a famous fence
builder.

La Bonita we moved to San Simón. The *patrón* of the rancho in
San Simón was a man by the name of Mr. Wilson, who knew my
husband from the time he was a child because Sra. Montoya had
cooked for him up in Mascot. In San Simón my husband was *el*
caporal—the foreman in charge of the rancho. It was a sheep
ranch, and he was in charge of the shepherds, the workers, and
the fields. He used to take mule trains of supplies to the shepherds
in remote parts of the mountains. It was a large ranch—four sections I believe—thousands of sheep. I remember that suddenly
and without warning the sheep were driven by the ranch to drink
water, and the string of sheep stretched from the road all the way
to the ranch house, as far as the eye could see.

When we were at San Simón I also did the washing and ironing for the owners of the ranch. How they loved the way I ironed!
Everywhere I went, people wanted me to do the ironing.

After we left San Simón we moved to the Sierra Linda Ranch in the mountains near Sonoita. It was a guest ranch owned by an American woman. My husband worked as a wrangler; he took the guests out on horseback rides. He did other jobs as well. They had a herd of cows, and he milked them so the guests would have fresh milk.

There was a time when I washed and ironed for all the guests at the Sierra Linda Ranch. American children would go up there for their Christmas and summer vacations. Sometimes there were as many as fifteen children. I washed and ironed for all of them. I worked as hard as my husband did. When the children came home from school, I would stop to make them dinner and then continue with the ironing. I ironed and ironed and ironed until I was finished. *Parada* (standing). *Sás y sás y sás con esa plancha.* (At it and at it and at it with that iron.)

We came to Tubac in 1943 because, as I have told you, my husband was a famous builder of fences. Mr. Bowman, who was a very important and wealthy man from the Nogales area, owned a lot of property in this valley; my husband built fences all over this area, from here all the way to Aguirre's Ranch in El Colorado (Red Rock). I tell you, he made a circle of fences around this state from Redington to La Bonita to San Simón to Sonoita to Tubac to Arivaca to El Colorado!

Even in Tubac I was famous for my *planchada* (ironing), and people kept after me to wash and iron, so I did. When we came here, we bought a little plot of land—about two acres with an old house. My oldest son, Julio, lives next door to me now; my daughter Rita Ybarra across the alley; and my daughter Barbara Solares just down the way. We were the first in Tubac to sell to an Americano. We sold the house to Dale Nichols in 1968. He was an artist and a very nice man. When we first came to Tubac it was *pura Mexicanada*; now it is *puro Americano*. I don't get out much, not even to see the neighbors anymore. Anyway, I don't speak English, so what's the use.

Socorro Félix Delgado

MY NAME IS SOCORRO DELGADO. I was born on September 9, 1920, in Tucson at my grandparents' home at 443 S. Meyer. My parents' names were José Delgado and Carlota Félix Delgado. My mother was born in Tucson on December 26, 1892, and died in 1985 at the age of ninety-three. My father was from the area of San Ignacio and Magdalena, Sonora; he came to Tucson as a young man to find work. My maternal grandparents' names were Jesús Félix and Andrea Arreola Félix. My grandmother Andrea, Manina we called her, was born in Ures, Sonora, in 1871; she came to Tucson when she was three years old and died in 1968 at the age of ninety-seven in her home at 447 S. Meyer. My grandfather Jesús was from Pitiquito, Sonora. I remember *his* mother—my great-grandmother. Her name was Apolonia Félix; we called her Grande. She had come from Spain, and when I was little she was already very *ancianita*. She died in 1934 at the age of 103! My grandfather was her only child, and, you know, in those days the older people stayed with the family. I lived with my grandmother Andrea when I was growing up, and at one time we had four generations living in our house at the same time.

My great-grandmother Grande was a seamstress. She was very independent and liked to work and earn her own money. She even left for California once to do sewing; she was told she could earn a lot of money there. When she came back she brought a railroad car full of furniture and china and pictures, some of which I still have in my apartment. The first house my grandparents bought was at 443 S. Meyer. It was big—five or six bedrooms. Grande had her own sewing room in that house. She used her bedroom as a fitting room—I remember the mannequin. She made dresses for the whole wedding party, the *madrinas* (bridesmaids), and for the flower girls, as well as the bride. She also knew how to crochet; she embroidered. She did *deshilado*. That is an old-fashioned needlework where you pull the threads in cloth. She had a wooden frame for stretching the cloth. She pulled the threads (woof) and gathered the other threads (warp) into a design using a needle. She did needlepoint and made pillows for

Carlota Félix and José Delgado, parents of
Socorro, 1919.

chairs out of velveteen and colorful yarn. I still have a little cush-
ion that she made. She would order from a catalogue, and the
needlepoint would come in a kit—the pattern, the different col-
ored yarns, the instructions. There's a lady still living, Herminia
Trujillo Moreno, who remembers well going to my great-
grandmother for lessons.

Grande used to sew for us kids. When I graduated from the
eighth grade at St. Augustine Cathedral School, the old Marist
College on Ochoa, she made me my graduation dress—silk or-
gandy, pale pink, with a big sash. She was already over one hundred years old when she made me that dress.

My mother told me that before she was married, she remembers my great-grandmother playing a card game with different
ladies who came to the house. Señora Carrillo, Leo's (Sr.) grand-

mother, and Señora Amado. She remembered because she used to fix coffee and little snacks to serve the ladies while they were playing. It was an old-fashioned card game that Mexican ladies used to play called "Malia."

The day she died I was in the house. My mother and grandmother always went to mass at the cathedral—every day, rain or shine. They asked me if I wanted to stay with Grande. They told me that if she had trouble breathing to give her a little spoonful of water. So I sat with her; I didn't want to leave her side because I was afraid that something might happen to her. I guess she was dying, but I didn't know it. I could see her hand moving over the ribbon trim on the blanket, and I asked myself, "What is she doing?" She always made me thread needles for her because she could not see too well; she made me thread a needle on the very day that she died because she could feel that a thread was unraveling on her blanket and she wanted to make it right. That's the kind of person she was.

I remember that she was constantly at her machine—an old Singer treadle. She would get up in the morning and sit at her machine before breakfast, and Manina used to have me go and get her and help her up so she could come to eat. She had sat so long at her sewing machine through all those years that when she got up she was all bent over her cane.

I never liked to sew—she did teach me to embroider, that's about it! I liked to play baseball with the boys outside, and she'd have a fit when she'd see me jumping around like a tomboy. But she tried. I can remember all the things she made because I would sit on the floor and watch her. I would come in all sweaty from playing and sit on the *petates* (grass mats) that her relatives in Pitiquito used to make for her from palm trees. The petate was cool and she used it in her sewing room to keep threads and material from falling on the floor. People would come and buy her things. The house was always full of people. And do you know what they stole when they broke into the house before I sold it? Her sewing machine!

When my grandparents Andrea and Jesús were first married, they lived over at the Baboquívari at the King's Ranch. My grandfather was Mr. Manuel King's main vaquero. That was the number one King, the *original* King. My grandmother went there as a young bride at the age of about sixteen or seventeen knowing nothing. She had been the smallest in the family and also raised by *her* grandmother, and she didn't know how to cook or wash or do anything. There were other women there—the wives of other *vaqueros*—and she would go and talk to them, but she was also very proud and independent and didn't like to admit that she didn't know how to cook. She would say, "And how do you make *albóndigas* (meatball soup)? How do you make this? How do you make that?" "Well, there's nothing to it," they would tell her. "Everybody does it the same way." "Yes, but how do *you* make them?" she would ask, and then she would run to her house and write it down before she forgot it.

My grandmother used to tell me about how Margarita (Corra) King would come and visit her; Margarita must have been very independent also because she lived at the Baboquívari by herself; she was *the* schoolteacher there. That's where she met Manuel King and later married him. Margarita was Mexicana also; she was from Hermosillo.

My grandmother told me that the Baboquívari was a very lonely place. She was so young and she was afraid. My grandfather would leave early in the morning and come back late at night while they were herding cattle.

This is how they got their farm. Someone was selling a farm in Sahuarito—I don't remember how much, but it was less than a thousand dollars. Jesús, my grandfather, said to her, "You know, Vieja, if we only had some money to give down, I could own my own place and I wouldn't have to work for anybody— quiero trabajar por si—quiero mi propio negocio." And she said, "Well, how much do you need?" And he told her two hundred dollars. And she said, "Oh, but I have two hundred." "Where?" "In a little coffee can." She was a good one to save money and my grandfather didn't know. And that's how they got their place, and my grandfather never worked for anybody again a single day of his life.

When he went with the down payment to see about buying the

ranch, she went and knelt in front of the Holy Family—it was a
little picture that *her* mother had given to her—and she prayed
that he would be able to buy it. She called the Holy Family "Los
Dulces Nombres"—"The Sweet Names" (Jesus, Mary, and Joseph). When it came true that they bought the ranch, every year
after that she would have a velación in honor of Los Dulces
Nombres on December 24.

The name of the ranch was La Providencia (Providence). It
was registered in the post office and the mailman delivered mail
there. It must have been a big place because when my Tío Francisco got married—he was the oldest son—they gave him half
and still had a big place.

There was an old house out there already when they moved
there; they added to it. One of the first things that my grandmother added to the house was a little room where she made her
chapel, and that is where all the saints and framed pictures that I
have began. A priest from the cathedral in Tucson—it was the
only church in town in those days—used to go on Saturdays, and
they would line up and he would hear confessions. On Sunday
the priest would say mass and all the neighbors from all the
ranches would come. My grandparents would put a little cot for
the priest in the chapel because that was the only extra room, and
that is where he spent the night.

My grandmother had lots of pictures in that chapel. A big
Holy Family that my niece has now and a Santo Niño de Atocha
in a gold-colored frame, and a large picture of the Blessed
Mother with the Little Child, and umpteen little ones—little stat-
ues of every saint. My grandmother also had San Isidro Labrador
on the rancho because he is the patron saint of farmers and ranchers. It was a black and white picture; the saint was kneeling.
When she moved into town she had the four walls of her bedroom covered with pictures of saints.

The chapel had a door going to the outside and there was a garden there—El Jardín she called it. And there were lots of flowers
and vines and an arbor, and lots of roses.

I remember the ranch house well because I lived there until I
was about five years old; my father and mother moved out there

*Andrea "Manina" Félix, maternal grandmother
of Socorro, with Socorro's cousin Francisco
"Pepe" Félix, ca. 1900.*

after they were married. When my grandfather Jesús died in
1926, I came into town to keep my grandmother company, but I
used to go and visit my parents out there. I remember a long living room—a *sala*—as you came into the house. At one end of the
sala was a little door that led to the chapel, and at the other end
there was another door that led into a big bedroom and then a
smaller one. There were no hallways. Next to the sala there was
a long, long kitchen; there was no dining room. They ate at a dining table in the kitchen, and there was a big wood stove there
also—*grandota*. And I remember a big gate—*puertón lo decíamos*—
because when my Panino—my grandfather—came in from town
I would run—*de chiquita*—and try to open it for him, and I
couldn't even reach the lock.

My mother told me that she and her brothers went to school
in a horse-drawn buggy—*el boguecito*. My mother and another
little girl would sit in the back, and my uncles Ramón and Francisco would sit in the front and drive. They went to school in Sahuarito. There was a one-room schoolhouse there. There was an
acequia, too, and they'd give the horse water and then put him

out to pasture while they were in school. Many years later when el paseo (rodeo parade) started, my grandmother loaned that boguecito to the parade people, but I don't know what ever happened to it.

My mother was always very hardworking, even as a child. She would get up real early in the morning and wash the dishes in a tina. They had to draw water from a well because they had no sink. She'd make little baking powder biscuits from scratch every morning for herself and her brothers, and they would take sandwiches to school. She made tortillas early in the morning when she was very young also. She made burritos and they took them to school for lunch. She made breakfast. They always had potatoes scrambled with eggs. It took a lot of time to cook because they made everything from scratch. If they were going to make a caldo, they had to go out and pick the vegetables in the garden, the corn, squash, carrots, potatoes, and they had to wash everything real well. I remember my mother saying, "What's to it (cooking) now that all this prepared food has come into being? Everything is in the refrigerator and freezer!" They roasted their own coffee beans—I did that, too—in a big pan on top of the stove until they browned to a certain color and it smelled very good. They stored the roasted coffee in a can and ground it fresh whenever they made coffee. They boiled the grounds in water and then filtered it. My mother and Manina made such wonderful coffee.

Of course, they had the carne seca. They put it in the oven to roast it a little bit, soaked it, and then pounded it to make carne machaca. This is what they did in their "spare time." They stored the meat in their "refrigerator"—a cabinet with screen that they would put outside in the fresh air. And then they would fry the machaca with potatoes or eggs.

Workers on my grandfather's farm made the sartas (strings of chile), but my mother and grandmother would take the chile from the sartas and clean it well—not wet it, but wipe it dry with a clean dish towel. They roasted it in the oven—all this was done with mesquite wood—in that big stove. Then they took it outside to let it cool and dry well. I did that, too. And then they ground the chile with a hand grinder and covered it and had the chile ready. All this had to be done after the evening meal—roast the coffee, ground the chili, and pound the meat.

My mother was a very good housekeeper, even as a little girl living on the ranch. She cleaned the whole sala—she remembered that it took all afternoon. "I started with the living room after lunch and when I finished it was time for supper," she used to tell me. When she was older she always wore a big apron, the kind that covers you in the front and the back. She had a little cloth that she kept in the pocket, and she was forever dusting things as she passed by. She'd come out of her bedroom in the morning with that apron on. I rarely saw her without it. I used to tease her that she slept in that apron.

Her brothers were always outside working with their fathers as cowboys. My grandfather was very fond of his sons. He bought them beautiful black horses. He had silver bridles and spurs made for them in Nogales. Their saddles were all tooled leather, made by hand. And what boots they had! Everything was done on horseback—they went to visit their *novias* (sweethearts), went to visit other ranchos and ran errands. They used to come to Tucson by horse and wagon. Later they got one of the first cars—my grandmother called it "El Dodgie."

My grandfather had horses and cattle, and they used to butcher their own cattle and make carne seca. They had all kinds of vegetables—oodles of corn, green onion, squash, *cilantro*, tomatoes, and beans. They used to sell that. They sacked the beans in one-hundred-pound sacks. My grandfather had workers from Mexico working for him, and he had little houses there for the workers. To the day she died my grandmother used to have a little trellis in her backyard in town where she had a grapevine. She grew tomato, *manzanilla* (camomile), *cilantro*, and green onion. She had a fig tree and *nopales* (prickly pear) and geraniums.

I remember the trees. There was a big apricot tree there, and we used to knock down the apricots we could reach with a stick. And the mulberry trees, oh, how they scolded us when we got the berry juice on our dresses! And the pomegranates, and great big mesquite trees and *tápiros* (elderberry trees)! My grandmother used to make a tea out of the mesquite bark; she washed it real well and chopped it up and boiled it. It was for a fever. It worked like a laxative. She used the flower from the tápiro—it was called *sauco*—and she dried the flower and put it in little jars to make a tea when we had the flu. She collected and dried *negrita*, which was also a little bark, and manzanilla, and *hierba manzo*, and she made teas with them. Negrita was used for stomachaches and manzanilla was given to babies for colic. She had a lot of roses and she dried the rose hips and put them in little jars and in the summer she made a real refreshing tea. It is called *rosa de castilla* in Spanish.

Manzanilla was good hot or cold. We'd take our bath and then come in and have some tea and then take a nap. "How dare you not take a nap! If you don't want to sleep, that's all right; just rest so you won't be out there in the sun." When we lived on South Meyer she made manzanilla and put it in an icebox. Panino put a sign in the window that had the numbers twenty-five, fifty for the amount of ice you wanted. Mr. Fisher, the iceman, got down from his wagon and brought it in on his shoulder, and there he would go, dripping through the house to the icebox on the back porch.

Even after I had moved to my apartment and my Manina had been dead I don't know how many years, I found little jars with her herbs on the shelves of the cabinet.

After the ranch was sold, my parents moved to Tempe where my father worked as foreman on a farm. When my grandfather died, I lived with my grandmother in town to keep her company. Later, when my parents moved, I stayed with her because I was going to St. Joseph's Academy. So I was raised by my grandmother—*por eso aprendí de ella* (that's why I learned so much from her).

My grandmother was very religious. She told us that she was raised by *her* grandmother and that *she* was also very religious and that's where she learned all this. Her grandmother's name was Lolita and she used to call her Malita.

My grandmother had a special devotion to the rosary, and we used to pray the rosary every night, on our knees. And after the rosary she prayed to each and every saint whose picture she had up there on her wall. So when she would say, "Let's pray the rosary," I used to think, "Oh, no!" because it would take forever! And we had to stay on our knees. If we dared to squirm or slouch she would give us "that look"—straighten up, keep still, stay quiet.

As I have said, she had a *velación* in thanksgiving to Los Dulces Nombres because they had granted her prayer when they wanted to buy the ranch. She had the velación from the first year they moved to the ranch. My mother told me they would be a whole week in preparing for it. So Christmas was always very special to her because, although people would say, "That's not the day of the Holy Family," she would say "That's the day the baby was born." She always had this little altar, a little statue of Los Dulces Nombres which I still have and the two candles. But on Christmas Eve she would dress it up special. She covered the little table with beautiful crocheted and embroidered cloths that my great-grandmother had made. For many years I helped her decorate. We hung sheets on the wall and pinned a lot of paper flowers on them. She made the flowers herself. And in the backyard we had a big palm tree. She would have somebody cut the palm fronds, and we cleaned them and put them this way and that way. And then she would buy four *big* candles at the cathedral and put two on each side of Los Dulces Nombres. I used to buy things at Kress'—little birds and little bells—anything to hang to make it more colorful. And Manina would supervise and make sure that everything was done just so, that everything matched, that nothing was crooked. When we finished, she would say, "Tenemos que tener los claveles frescos." She would always buy six fresh carnations to put on the altar. It was a *big* spending.

The important thing was the family. My parents, my sisters, Carmen and Andrea, and my brother, José, my uncles and aunts and cousins and neighbors and friends also came to my grandmother's house early on the twenty-fourth. Christmas Eve was a day of abstinence—you don't eat meat—so they made enchiladas and potato salad with egg. And she made biscochuelos and wine out of dried figs. She fermented the figs in a big crock, covered it with a clean dish towel, stirred it on different days, and put it in little bottles. That was a special treat on the night of the twenty-fourth. When people arrived they had a little snack, and then we went into her room to pray. The rosary was the important thing. After the rosary we had hymns, and she said special prayers:

Jesús, José y María	Jesus, Joseph, and Mary,
Les doy el corazón	I give you my heart
Y el alma mía	And my soul
Jesús, José y María	Jesus, Joseph, and Mary,
Encomiendo a toda mi	I commend my family to
familia.	you.
Jesús, José y María	Jesus, Joseph, and Mary,
Que me asistan en mi última	Help me in my final agony.
agonía.	

To St. Francis she prayed:

Seráfico San Francisco	Seraphic St. Francis,
Siervo querido de Dios	Beloved servant of God
Te pido por las cinco llagas	I ask, through the five
	wounds
Que el Señor oprimió en Vos.	That our Lord bestowed on
	you
Que nos des una corta	That you give us a small
limosna	offering
De nuestra salvación	For our salvation
Por amor de Dios.	For the love of God.

And we would answer, "Por amor de Dios." She knew many more verses and recited them, and we repeated the refrain, "Por amor de Dios." And to the Sacred Heart she prayed:

O Corazón Sagrado	Oh, Sacred Heart,
Manantiel de protección	Mantle of protection,
En ti Senor he confiado	In You, Lord, I have trusted
No desprecies mi oración	Do not disregard my prayers
Remedia, Dueño Adorado	And remedy, Beloved Master,
Mi amarga tribulación.	My bitter tribulation.

And then she sang. My grandmother had a very beautiful voice.

Daremos gracias con fe	We give thanks with faith
Y crecidas esperanzas	And growing hope
Cantando las alabanzas	Singing the praises
De Jesús, María y José.	Of Jesus, Mary, and Joseph.

We sang to the Blessed Mother.

O María, Madre mía	Oh, Mary, Mother of mine,
O Consuelo del mortal	Oh, the consolation of mortals,
Aparadme y guiadme	Help me and guide me
A la patria celestial.	To the celestial land.

There was a prayer that she said and we all had to answer:

Manina: ¿Quién en esta casa nos da luz?
Todos: ¡Jesús!
Manina: ¿Quién la llena de alegría?
Todos: ¡María!
Manina: ¿Quién la conserva en la fe?
Todos: ¡José!
Manina: Pues muy confiada estaré
           Llevando en mi casa
           Jesús, María y José.

Manina: Who in this house gives light?
ALL: JESUS!
Manina: Who fills it with happiness?
ALL: MARY!
Manina: Who preserves it in faith?
ALL: JOSEPH!
Manina: Then confident I'll be
         Having in my house
         Jesus, Mary, and Joseph.

If we didn't answer loudly enough she made us do it over.

About ten o'clock we would have a break and eat enchiladas, salad, biscochuelos, and some fruit. She passed around the fig wine in little goblets on silver and crystal platters. That wine was very exquisite. When my sister and I got older, we did that.

Manina had a little notebook with songs, and she taught them to us and made us practice, so that if other people came we would know the songs. We giggled when we practiced, and she would tell us to stop. We had to get up in front of the people and recite little poems:

Viva el sol	Long live the sun;
Viva la luna	Long live the moon;
Viva el arco iris de la fe	Long live the rainbow of faith;
Vivan todos los devotos	Long live all the devotees
De Jesús, María, y José.	Of Jesus, Mary, and Joseph.

The waiting was till twelve, and then at midnight everybody went to see the Baby Jesus in the middle of the table; she had a cute little manger, and we went two by two, starting with the children, to adore the Baby Jesus. She sang a special little song that went something like this:

Vénganse todos los niños
(O las niñas o las damas o los hombres)
En un número infinito
A adorar este niño chiquito este niño bendito.
Vénganse a adorar al Niño Jesús
Que nos llena con Su gracia y con Su luz.
O vénganse a la adoración. (Se repite tres veces)

Gather together all ye children (or ladies or gentlemen)
In an infinite number;
To adore this small Child, this blessed Child.
Oh, come let us adore the Child Jesus
Who fills us with His Grace and with His Light.
Oh, come to the adoration. (Repeat three times)

Under the little altar table she had hidden little gifts—a little doll or a little car or some candy from the dime store. She told us that the Baby Jesus had left it there because we had been good. We didn't know Christmas trees; we didn't know Santa Claus.

My cousins wanted to stay when the adults went home and Manina put this great big quilt in the living room, and she put pillows all around. The girls slept on the floor in the sala and the boys on the enclosed back porch.

When my grandparents first moved into town they bought a big house. There were five or six bedrooms in that old house. In 1925, after their children had married, they built a smaller home next door. My grandfather helped make the adobes out back. My grandparents rented the rooms in the old house, and Grandfather had other little *casitas* around the block, which he rented. His father had left him some acres in Pitiquito, which he also rented. After my grandfather died, my grandmother continued with the rentals, and that is how she made her living. When I was older, I went with her to Nogales to pick up the check from Pitiquito. She was a businesswoman in her little way. She took care of the rentals. She had me buy her receipt books. She went to school for about three years with the St. Joseph's sisters who came to Tucson from California. They had an *escuelita* and that is where she learned to read and write and count. Later, there was welfare, of course, but she never wanted any help. When she died, she had a little savings, enough for her funeral. She was a very *Cristiana*—everybody loved her. She used to tell me about her life, and she would say: "Don't just ask God for help; you have to do your part; don't just sit and wait for things to come from Over There." And she taught me to always be kind to people; it didn't matter who came to the door. "Even if you don't have anything, if it's a real hot day, then give them a cold glass of water and people will say, 'It's good!' And if it's cold and you don't have any coffee, just heat some water." And she told me, "Remember that there is only one God, and He is my Father and He is your Father and He is the Father of the drunk man going by and the Father of that little *viejita* (elderly woman) who is sick, so that makes us all brothers. So always be kind to people, no matter who they are."

At that time there were no rest homes, and the older people stayed with their family and died at home. The family came running to my grandmother. "Andreita, Andreita, my mother says to come because my father is very sick!" It was all a neighborhood thing there on Meyer Street—everybody knew each other—and she would take her rosary and go and pray. She walked everywhere. She said that a person who was dying was in great need of prayer because the devil was always around trying to tempt them even on their deathbed. She prayed to help them die peacefully. I remember once a little girl ran and said, "Andreita, come quick, quick." Manina ran with her apron still on. She not only prayed but also was very good at counseling and comforting people.

She also said the rosary at the *velorio*—the night before the burial. In those days they used to do that in the homes with the casket. They did it that way for my grandfather and my Tío Ramón, and for my great-grandmother, *esa viejita*, Apolonia. After the funeral there was the *novenario*—nine days of the rosary—at the family's house. She liked to begin the novenario on a Monday so that she had two Mondays during the nine days because she said that Monday was the day of souls in purgatory. She had a little prayer she said at the novenario:

> Por las ánimas benditas
> Todos hemos de rogar
> Que Dios las saque de penas
> Y las lleva a descansar.

> For the blessed souls
> We all should implore
> That God remove them from their suffering
> And take them to their rest.

She knew three generations of Carrillos at the mortuary. In those days the priests and deacons didn't say the rosary like they do now, and Arturo Carrillo, the father of Leo, Sr., used to come and get her. She made many friends like that. They never forgot her because she had prayed for them and she used never to charge for anything.   .

And oh! My mother was so different! She was serious and very shy, and when she finished cleaning up the kitchen—it would take her forever—she would peek around the corner and if there were people at the house she would go to her room and do her crocheting or work on her quilts and pray by herself. But I am like my grandmother—very outgoing.

We used to go to the Molina family's ranch. They'd send their sons to get my grandmother to say the rosary for the velación de la Virgen de Guadalupe on December 12. They had a ranch up there by Sabino Canyon, and Francisco and Josefa, the parents of Gilbert and María, the first owners of the Casa Molina, would give thanks to the Virgen because it was through *her* that their children had that little ranch and restaurant. And the Blessed Mother is *still* blessing that family! They had a very large Virgen de Guadalupe in a frame and they decorated it with fresh flowers all around.

My grandmother prayed a very beautiful rosary and María,

the Molinas' daughter, sang; she had a very beautiful voice. They said other prayers also and talked and we had dinner. Then we prayed and sang again. All night long. In the morning we had breakfast. They were in the kitchen the whole time cooking. So I guess you can say I ate at the *real* Casa Molina.

My grandmother was always very active in the church. She knew three generations of bishops. She remembered when Bishop Gercke came in 1924. She went to the reception that they had for him at the university in the old auditorium. Way back, when she still lived at La Providencia, she went around to the ranchos collecting money for the first San Augustín Church—they were remodeling. She said that there was this lady who told her, "Andrea, I don't have any money, but I have these two chickens. Do you want to take them and sell them?" And she said yes. That's the way it was. She ended up with I don't know how many chickens because *she* bought them and then donated that money to the church. She used to go around with my uncle in that boquecito—who could tell her no!

After she moved into town she always belonged to the cathedral. Back in those days it was the ladies who had the St. Vincent de Paul Society. My grandmother did that. Padre Pedro Timmermans gave them money and they bought groceries and filled little boxes with food to give to the poor people who came to the rectory asking for food.

She was a *veladora*—she belonged to the Society of Perpetual Light. They had adoration every day so that the Blessed Sacrament was not alone. Margarita King and Concepción Rebeil also belonged to that society. My grandmother was also a *celadora*—there was a day in the month that she was responsible for twelve ladies who would come from six in the morning until six at night. My grandmother used to stay all day in case someone didn't show up. We were in school, and we loved that day because she took lunch—little burros and things from the Trujillos' Guaymense Bakery.

When school was out at noon we ran and had lunch with her! They don't have the veladoras anymore. All those things have ended.

She used to give me her blessing when I went out, and in all the years that she lived while I was working, I never missed a *bendición*, even when I was running late. My cousins and friends came by sometimes when they were going on a trip or out of town or on a picnic and she would give them the bendición. She said, "En el nombre del Padre y del Hijo y del Espíritu Santo. Que Dios los bendiga." ("In the name of the Father and the Son and the Holy Ghost. May God bless you.") She would place her hands on our heads and then give us a hug.

When the Second World War started, my brother José, my brother-in-law, my cousins, and my cousins' husbands served. At one time there were as many as fifteen of our immediate family who had gone to war! Every Friday Father Burns and Father Rossetti had a novena for the Sorrowful Mother. We would go and mention the names of the boys who were in the war. There was a victory candelabra with seven candles, and the candles would be lit. They lasted for a week. People came to my grandmother also and asked her to pray for their sons. Many were killed, but no one from our family was killed. My grandmother wanted to do something in thanksgiving for those who had come home safely, so she got together the families. Monseñor Timmermans gave us his blessing, and we made a procession to San Xavier Mission. I remember it was hot; we were all perspiring. We walked all the way! It was all open in those days; there were farms, milpas—nothing was fenced. I remember we had to cross acequias with running water. It's so different now! When we got to the mission we walked to El Cerrito where there was a grotto to the Blessed Mother. We prayed the rosary there in thanksgiving.

In those days, too, they had the Month of May at the cathedral to honor the Blessed Mother. Certain families had a day that they were responsible for buying flowers and decorating the altar; they were also responsible for mass the following day. From the time I was a little girl—first my grandmother and then my mother—our day was May 11. My grandmother came in the morning and we had lunch with her and helped her decorate. We bought fresh flowers from a lady who used to grow and sell them.

Andrea, José, and Socorro Delgado at their First
Communion, ca. 1929. The girls' dresses were made
from the wedding dress of their mother.

We washed the vases and made the bouquets ourselves. Mrs.
Tapia was my grandmother's partner, and when she died, then
Lucy Tapia Disenz took over. We still decorate on May 11 to this
day—Lucy, my sister Andrea, and I—but now we buy the bouquets already made.

Padre Pedro Timmermans had a rosary each evening in May.
At the end of each mystery of the rosary, there was a procession
where all the little girls dressed in white and offered flowers to the
Blessed Mother. On the last day of May there was a crowning of
the Blessed Mother. But all that died out. I guess it's just too
much for people now.

I belonged to the Sodality—Las Hijas de María—for many

Socorro Félix Delgado, far left, and Sophie Salazar Miles, far right, *with flower girls at Month of May Procession, St. Augustine Cathedral, ca. 1940.*

years. We were a group of single girls who honored the Blessed Mother. We processed on her feast days—August 15 (the Assumption), December 8 (the Immaculate Conception), and during May. The whole month of May we dressed in white and wore little veils and went to the cathedral to be in charge of the little girls who were offering flowers in the procession. When we were young, my sisters and I did the same, and other young ladies took care of us. Lolita Aros used to sing "Bring Flowers of the Fairest." She sang the Hail Mary at the three beads at the end of the rosary—that's the Mexican rosary. And the little girls would sing, "Santa María, Madre de Dios." But there is no more Sodality either.

My grandmother came here when she was three years old and all her life, because God had granted her so many blessings, she wanted to go visit the Virgen de Guadalupe in the Basilica in

Mexico City. My cousins and I took her when she was seventy-five years old. She never got tired or sick the whole time. I have never seen anyone so happy, and the first time I ever saw her cry was when she saw la Virgen for the first time. When she knew we were going to take her, she went to Jacome's and bought herself a beautiful navy-blue dress out of georgette to wear on the day we went to the Basilica. She never wore that dress again, until twenty-two years later when she died. She kept everything she had worn on that trip—the stockings, underwear, and a little veil in a box on the top shelf of the wardrobe. She took it out from time to time to air it or send it to cleaners. On the day of her funeral, something very odd happened; the funeral car that always went down Main to the cemetery took a turn and went around the block in front of Holy Family Church on West 3rd Street. Everyone was wondering: "*What* is he doing." "¿Está loco?" Later Leo Carrillo (Sr.) told me that my grandmother had asked him to drive her by the front of Holy Family Church, because it was dedicated to Los Dulces Nombres, and he had remembered at the last minute.

I had never worked in all those years. I was happy keeping my grandmother company and accompanying her on all her charities.

It was Christmas; I was twenty-nine years old, and I had already been thinking about it. My mother and father had come for the velación, and my father noticed that I was quiet and looking out the window. I had been thinking, "What will I do when they are gone?" My father asked me, "What are you thinking?" And then I told him that maybe I should look for a job, that I was getting older and was not married and it would get harder to get a job. He said, "Why do you want to work? You are not used to it; you don't know what it is to have to get up in the morning and go out of the house and be told what to do. You'll never be happy again. Do you need money?" "No." "Then what do you need?" I explained it to him as well as I could; I couldn't really explain it to myself either. Maybe God was trying to tell me something. My father told me to sleep on it, and then the next morning he asked me if I was still thinking about getting a job, and I said yes. "Ah," he said, "wait until I die; then you can go to work." And do you know, he died the following January. My brother-in-law had a niece who worked at the hospital, and I had gone to their house to visit their sick mother. The niece told me that they needed someone at St. Mary's Hospital to replace a girl who was going on vacation. I don't remember ever filling out an application. When the sister asked me where I had worked, I told her that I had never worked. "You've never worked! Oh, well, then we can train you the way we want." They put me to work in the dietician's office. They sent me to the university to take a course in nutrition. I thought to myself, "I will try this on a two-week basis." I was so tired those first days because I was not used to it! Anyway, I ended up staying for thirty-five years! I was very happy working. I got to know so many people! Now I have a little retirement. Don't you think that God helped me? Because in the old days you could get by with any little thing, but not anymore. When I first started to work I was getting forty-two dollars every two weeks, but that was enough because I was living with my grandmother and buying next to nothing, just the extras.

Since my retirement in 1984 I have dedicated myself to people. I am a Eucharistic minister at the hospital. I belong to the Catholic Daughters of America. I help the nurse at the Wellness Clinic at the Casa Encanto Senior Citizens Home once a week. I do intake paperwork, but I help most with the translating. There are many older people who only speak Spanish. I am not bored. I have my family and friends; there is always a wedding or baptism. Some of my friends from Las Hijas de María have grandchildren now. There is always something.

My mother and I lived in my grandmother's house at 447 S. Meyer until 1985. From about 1980 Mr. Kelly Rollings kept saying to me, "Sell me the house, Socorro; sell me the house. If you sell me the house I will let you live in it for nothing for as long as you want." But I didn't want to sell while my mother was living; she was not well, and I did not want to move her to a strange place. But one day after I had gone out—about eleven o'clock in the morning—someone broke into the house and robbed us. Can you imagine, my mother ninety-three years old and sick in bed! So I got very scared and the very next week I went to see Mr. Rollings and told him that I would sell. My mother and I moved to a house on West Congress that belonged to one of my relatives. My mother only lived for about three more months after we moved. So now I live in this little apartment. My sister Andrea said, "It's so small!" But I don't mind. I like it.

Carmen Celia Beltrán

MY NAME IS CARMEN CELIA BELTRÁN. I was born in the state of Durango, Mexico, in the hacienda El Salto near the capital city, which was also called Durango. I was born during the turbulent years that preceded the revolution of Mexico of 1910. My father's name was Vicente Beltrán, and my mother's name was Guadalupe Martínez Beltrán. My father was a composer, a band and orchestra director, and professor of music.

Because of my father's political involvement, many times our family had to hide in the mountains or travel a long way on horseback. I was very young and in poor health, so when I was about two years old I was taken to a Carmelite Convent in Durango. I learned very fast, and when my parents had settled in the city and I was of age to attend public school, I was admitted to the third grade. Games and entertainment did not interest me; I was very studious and only cared for reading and the theater.

By the time I was eleven years old, I had already finished elementary and intermediate school. This presented quite a problem. There were only two colleges in Durango—a two-year business college and the state teachers' college with a four-year course of study. The required age for admission was fifteen, but with special tests and recommendations, I was admitted. At the end of the first year, I received a prize.

It was very difficult for my family to continue living in Mexico, because of my father's activities. Although he had friendly relationships with the factions in both political parties, many dangerous incidents threatened his life. One such incident, which I find amusing, occurred when a group of military officers gathered to celebrate the promotion of one of their group to the rank of general. A medal in the shape of a cross was placed on the general's chest. Since my father was a teacher of music and literature to several of the general's companions, he was asked to give a toast on behalf of those gathered there. Having had a few *copitas* too many, many applauded when my father said:

*Carmen Celia Beltrán at the
age of sixteen.* Arizona
Historical Society Library:
Mexican Heritage Project.

"En tiempos de las bárbaras naciones
De las cruces colgaban los ladrones;
Hoy, estando en el 'Siglo de Las Luces'
A los ladrones se les cuelgan cruces."

"In times of the barbaric nations
Thieves were hung on crosses;
Now, during the 'Century of Enlightenment'
Crosses are hung on thieves."

Needless to say, it cost my father his freedom for a few days; he was sent to prison immediately.

Before the end of my second year in college, we had to leave the country. The director and other teachers tried to persuade my parents to leave me in Durango until I received my degree, but it was useless. Everything we owned was sold, and we started the trip which brought us to the United States.

A hold-up of the special train in which we were traveling caused quite a change in my father's plans. Making unavoidable stops in Monterrey, Nuevo León, and Laredo, Tamaulipas, we fi-

Carmen Celia Beltrán dancing with her brother,
Vicente Orlando, at a school benefit fundraiser, San
Antonio, Texas, ca. 1926. Arizona Historical
Society Library: Mexican Heritage Project.

nally reached San Antonio, Texas, where my maternal grandmother lived. My father established his music business in San
Antonio; under contract with the QRS Music Company of Chi-
cago, he made masters for player piano rolls.

My brother and I had to go to school without being able to
speak English; for me it was tragic to have to re-enter elementary
school. Fortunately, it did not take me long to learn English, and
I was transferred from first to third and then to sixth grade. I
graduated from high school with honors in 1924 and received a
scholarship.

When I graduated from high school, I worked full-time at a savings and loan association where I had worked part-time summers while a student. I enrolled in a business college to study shorthand, but instead I was employed to teach Spanish. I worked at the college three evenings a week and the remaining evenings for a Spanish publishing firm. There were a number of newspapers and magazines for the large Hispanic population of San Antonio, and I wrote for them, including the monthly magazine *La Tribuna de la Raza* and a weekly newspaper, *El Imparcial*. I also wrote articles for publications in Monterrey, Nuevo León (Mexico), and Los Angeles.

During those early years in San Antonio, I was also active in the theater. I belonged to a dramatic club, and sometimes I had the lead in plays. My brother Vicente Orlando was my dance partner. We performed together; we danced tangos, waltzes, and *danza apache*. But my mother was very strict; our theatrical performances were limited to church or school affairs; my brother was not only my dance partner, he was also my chaperone, and when my brother left, my theatrical activities were interrupted.

I was often invited to be part of a radio program welcoming a famous artist or intellectual visiting San Antonio; it was easy for me to meet musicians or composers who needed my father's services to write or arrange their songs, or to prepare them for publication or piano rolls. I still remember many beautiful songs which I have never heard again.

VEN

Ven a mi pobre cabaña
que suspira y te extraña
cuando faltas de ahí.

Ven, que te espera la
      hamaca
y las flores de albaca
no perfuman sin ti.

COME

Come to my poor cottage
which is lonely and misses you
when you are gone from it.

Come, for the hammock is
      waiting
and the sweet-basil flowers
Give no perfume without
      you there.

Ven, ven, amor,
que triste estoy;
sin ti no hay luz
ni alumbra el sol.

Si vuelves a mi cabaña
donde llora la caña
con suspiros de amor,

se abrirán todas las flores
y darán sus olores

los naranjos en flor.

Come, come, my love,
I am so blue;
Without you there is no light
and the sun does not shine.

If you return to my cottage
where the sugarcane weeps
With signs of love,

all the flowers will bloom
And the orange blossoms will
again
give out their perfume.

My knowledge of Spanish shorthand enabled me to get acquainted with famous personalities. I became the secretary-stenographer at important meetings of well-known politicians whose names have gone down in the history of Mexico. Although I never finished my study of advanced shorthand in English, I had very interesting jobs with what I knew. At one time I was employed by a law office in San Antonio. When an urgent matter of the federal government came up, I was borrowed from the law office while the investigation of the postmaster was being conducted. At one time during the trial, I even had a police escort when it was found that one of the persons attending the hearing was carrying a gun.

For a while I devoted all my time to writing. During that time I was married for a short time. I have two daughters, Norma Celia and Yolanda Irma Viesca-Arizpe. My mother helped me in the care of my two daughters; she raised them so that I could pursue my work as a bookkeeper and secretary, and my artistic and literary endeavors. My mother was an extraordinary woman. Her physical appearance was delicate and frail, but spiritually she was a pillar of strength. With her example I learned to face the storms of life without allowing their violence to weaken my will. My mother dedicated her entire life to the care of her home and her children. Although household duties left her little free time, she never neglected her innate artistic abilities; she crocheted, embroidered, and wove exquisitely. She knew how to play the mandolin, and before she was married she sang in the church choir. At those times it was the custom for *tertulias* (gatherings) to be held in Mexican homes for conversations and family closeness. She was always very active in this endeavor. The most valuable legacy my mother left me has been my deep religious faith, which has been for me a most powerful shield in the struggles of life. I have never stopped saying the prayers in Spanish that she taught me during my childhood days.

Gracias y alabanzas te doy, Gran Señor, admirando tu poder
Pues con el alma en el cuerpo me has dejado anochecer;
Por tu caridad y tu amor permíteme amanecer
En gracia y servicio tuyo y sin ofenderte, amen.

I thank and praise You, Lord, admiring your great power
With the soul within my body you have allowed me to see
    the sunset
because your kindness and love allow me to see the dawn
being in your service, with your grace, and not offending
    you.

Santo ángel de mi Guardia, relicario del Señor
Que de Dios has sido enviado para ser mi defensor
Suplícote, ángel bendito, por tu gracia y tu poder,
Que me logres defender de los lazos del maldito.

Holy Guardian Angel of mine, envoy of the Lord,
Sent by Him to be my protector,
I beg of you, blessed Angel, that with your grace and power
You succeed in saving me from all evil.

Con Dios me acuesto; con Dios me levanto.
Con la gracia de Dios y del Espíritu Santo.

In God's love I retire; in God's love I awake,
With the grace of God and that of the Holy Spirit.

I made frequent trips from San Antonio to Monterrey and Mexico City during those years to visit good friends; it was during one of those trips to Monterrey that I signed a contract for a tour on a Radio Cadena Nacional. My friend, Evita Quintanar, sang her own compositions, and I recited my poems on the same subject. We were quite successful with the tour and received excellent reviews.

In 1938, because of health problems, I had to leave San Antonio in search of a high and dry climate; Tucson was highly recommended. I was first invited to Tucson by Professor Carlos E. Ballesteros, whom I had met while organizing a benefit festival in San Antonio. I had invited Professor Ballesteros, a harpist, and Joel Quiñonez, a violinist, both residents of Tucson, to participate in the festival. I began to spend the winters here; by that time my mother and children had moved to California to be with the rest of the family, and I made frequent trips to see them. In 1942 I made Tucson my permanent residence.

As soon as I arrived in Tucson I was introduced to Fr. Carmelo Corbellà, O.C.D., the pastor of Holy Family Church. I also met Don Ricardo Fierro, director of the Spanish language newspaper *El Tucsonense* and Don Jacinto Orozco, founder and director of "La Hora Mexicana" on KVOA radio station. I began to write a social column in *El Tucsonense* and to do radio work with Don Jacinto on KVOA and with Don Isaac Aviña on KTUC. On KTUC I was in charge of a weekly program called "Theatre of the Air." On KVOA I produced the only Catholic program in Spanish in the state of Arizona. It consisted of religious meditations and included music, poems, and subjects approved by the local clergy and authorized by Bishop Daniel J. Gercke. Some of my favorite topics were "La Devoción a la Virgen del Carmen"; "El Escapulario"; "El Sacerdocio"; and "Los Sacramentos y la Iglesia." Other themes of my talks included *relatos* (stories) of the famous saints and doctors of the church, such as Santa Teresa de Jesús, the doctor and reformer of the Carmelite Order. I also gave programs relating to domestic and patriotic themes.

At that time, Tucson had a population of less than 35,000, and the Mexican people organized frequent festivals in Tucson as well as in neighboring towns and cities. A very pleasant memory for me is the presentation in Tolleson of a theatrical production for the benefit of the construction of a church dedicated to our Lady of Guadalupe. In Tucson, also, I was in charge of the initial fundraiser held in the old Plaza Theater for the construction of the chapel on West 29th Street dedicated also to the Virgin of Guadalupe. My first theatrical involvement in Tucson was in *La Pasion*, directed by Father Carmelo and presented at Safford school. Some of my other works that have been presented on the radio as well as on the stage include *Arrullo* and *La Cuna Vacia*, which contain Mother's Day themes, a historical review, *México Ayer y Hoy*, and works of a religious nature such as *En el Extranjero*, *La Virgen y Juan Diego*, *Cristo y el Sepulturero*, and *El Regalo de Navidad*.

At Holy Family Church we attempted to continue the theatrical activities begun by Father Carmelo, after he returned to Spain. We had the help of the Little Flower Club, the C.Y.O. (Catholic Youth Organization), and the *cofradías* (religious confraternities), such as La Semana Devota and Niño de Praga. For several years we were very successful; the church was always filled.

In one of the shows in which I was program organizer and director, as well as performer on the stage, we staged a soldier's farewell. The couple said good-bye very dramatically. The young man who wore a soldier's uniform did not know anything about military attire. I was the lady in the couple, and being much taller than the soldier, it was agreed that before the curtain opened I would take my shoes off so that I could put my arms around him and my head on his shoulder for the farewell. With the rush of checking into the following number on the program, I forgot to remove my shoes. I was already on the stage, complaining bitterly of the war, when the young man came on the scene and I noticed that he was wearing the *kepis* (soldier's hat) in a horizontal instead of vertical position; that made the public and me laugh quite a bit. The poor soldier did not know what to do, and it took me a little while to stop laughing and tell him to fix his hat. He finally did during the embrace, which lasted until I was able to continue with the dialogue. Only the people in the front seats noticed that there was much more laughing before the crying!

I remember one very amusing incident involving Father Eliseo and his assistant, who were both from Spain. In the month of September, to commemorate Mexico's Independence, we were presenting a theatrical show at the Holy Family Parish Hall, in which we included a patriotic play entitled *Viva la Libertad* (Long Live Freedom). Only a few actors were needed for the main cast, but in one of the most emotional scenes a large group of voices was required to cheer loudly at the moment when the Goddess of Liberty broke the chains of the enslaved country of Mexico. The group of men did not have to rehearse with the cast but were given instructions as to when they were to start cheering behind stage.

On the night of the performance, a group of men sat with the audience to wait for the signal, but they were so interested in the play that they did not notice when they were given the signal and did not realize it until they heard Father Eliseo and his assistant yelling with their strong Spanish accent, "Long live freedom. . . . Down with bad government. . . . Death to the gachupines. . . . ¡VIVA MÉXICO!"

The audience broke out in laughter, and the patriotic soldiers felt very badly because they were not on time for the cheering.

In addition to the theater and radio, my activities in Tucson have included being director of the monthly magazine *Arizona* for six years; columnist for the newspaper *La Voz*, seven years; co-editor of *Alianza* magazine and director during its last three years of existence. All of the publications mentioned were written in Spanish, but I also worked in papers printed in English, like the *Tucson Daily Reporter*, published by George H. Dalton, who named me its editor in 1952. For a short time I worked as bookkeeper and wrote a few items for the *Weekend Reporter*, a weekly publication.

I have held other jobs like being a secretary to lawyers, among them attorney Charles McPhee Wright and his associate attorney Samuel P. Goddard, Jr., who were in charge of matters pertaining to the Indian tribes of Arizona. I have also been interpreter for the Industrial Commission of Arizona and for some lawyers in private cases; I am frequently asked to do translations from English to Spanish and vice versa. In California my activities have been of a different nature; I have been programmed in poetry recitals at the Teatro Intimo, and the club Madrinas de Santa Marta frequently includes me in the entertainment during intermission at their meetings and banquets.

Several times in Texas and in Arizona I have been part of the committee for the organization of the patriotic celebrations of the Mexican people. Because I have never approved of the idea of having royalty included in the affairs related to the independence of Mexico, I wrote a historical pageant in 1952, *México Ayer y Hoy*, with narration and descriptive scenery, which was presented in the auditorium of Tucson High School with great success on September 15 of that year and was also staged in other theaters.

In this historical pageant I wanted to project the most typical aspects of the predominant environment during the three periods of history in Mexico (Aztec, Colonial, and Independent). In Aztec Mexico I had authentic theatrical scenery with some marvelous paintings of side altars, center pyramid, and idols. To the costumes I had to devote a lot of study and time so that the characters would portray the splendor and royalty of the special ceremonies. For the Colonial period we had Spanish dances and historical features.

The scenes of Independent Mexico included a variety of typical national and regional costumes, which I had to design and make, with the cooperation and help of outstanding cultural personalities of Tucson like members of the symphony, university teachers, and local artists who devoted many hours to the task without knowing much about the art of sewing. I had an idea of

Scene from a play Aztec and Modern Mexico, *written and produced by Carmen Celia Beltrán. She also researched, designed, and made the costumes.* Arizona Historical Society Library: Mexican Heritage Project.

what was needed because during my first years in Tucson I lived in the home of an excellent dressmaker from Sonora, Mexico, Dona María de Jesús Valencia.

Whenever my daughters were living with me, they always took part in the shows, which helped them to continue speaking Spanish and to adhere to Mexican customs and traditions.

For the customary festivities of December 12, I wrote a play with narration and dialogues of a historical and religious nature. For many years my play was presented by the Society of Our Lady of Guadalupe from St. Augustine's Cathedral in many places, including Tucson Community Center.

For the frequent shows I have organized in Arizona, generally staged in parochial halls of various churches, I needed material. For many years the only source available was the bookstore owned by the Díaz Pulido brothers, but they could not always provide the material needed. In such cases I would adapt the script of some play appropriate for our cast and frequently included a comic sketch which I wrote myself.

There was a need of material for radio programs also, plays of short duration and for small casts, so I wrote plays that have been presented on special occasions even in recent years. The personnel of KXEW Radio Fiesta presented *Cristo y el Sepulturero* on a Holy Thursday and *La Cuna Vacía* on a Mother's Day. At the request of some of my Mexican composer friends, I have written lyrics in English for some of their songs, like "Noche de Luna," "Vereda Tropical," "Tal Vez," "En mi Retiro," and "Luna Amiga," by Gonzalo Curiel, and some selections composed by Manuel Alvarez Maciste to be used in the musical background of some Hollywood films. For my own pleasure I have written Spanish lyrics for some songs that I like very much like "Always" by Irving Berlin, "Giannina Mia" by Rudolf Friml, "Barcarola" by Offenbach, and "Sweet Mystery of Life" and "Kiss Me Again" by Victor Herbert.

For my cooperation in some of the activities of the Mexican American Unity Council, relating to their project of founding a cultural center in Tucson, I was honored with their Humanitarian Award in 1984 at a testimonial organized by the Hispanic community. In 1984 I also received an Amistad plaque from the City of Tucson, recognizing my work at KUAT.

Now, in the sunset of my life, activities are very limited. At the present time I produce and host a weekly radio program, "Homenaje a la Música Mexicana," which began in 1981 on Radio Universidad, KUAT Public Radio, under the direction of Manuel Arcadia. In this program I include old-time music, biographical data on composers, and some data relating to special dates or events of historical or musical value.

My poems have been published in newspapers and magazines in Mexico and the United States and have been included in some anthologies. I have published two books of poetry, but only for my family and close friends. I have material for other books which I plan to publish if life, time, and other important factors permit it.

I am grateful for the recognition and honors bestowed on me. They are a diamond brooch among the links of gold, the chain of very pleasant events that my life in Tucson has always been.

CANCIÓN

Poem by Carmen Celia Beltrán

¡MADRE MÍA! (1925)

    Una ofrenda de amor para ti canta
la voz del corazón en este día
en que la luz del cielo se abrillanta
cuando beso tu frente, ¡Madre mía!

    ¿Qué más puedo pedir? Mi dicha es tanta
Que nada hay comparable a mi alegría
porque tu estás conmigo, Madre santa,
y me amparan tus brazos todavía.

    Tus piadosas ternuras maternales
alivian mis heridas; tú deseas
que mi planta no sangren las espinas
aunque vaya corriendo entre zarzales.

    Tú, que todos mis sueños adivinas,
Madre, fuente de amor, bendita seas.

EN EL ANIVERSARIO DE SU MUERTE (1940)

    Hoy que no estás conmigo, Madre santa,
en mi hogar ya no hay cantos de alegría
y mi gran sufrimiento se agiganta
cuando en vano te busco, ¡Madre mía!

    Porque lejos de ti, mi pena es tanta
que me invade letal melancolía,
y empolvada mi lira, solo canta
del dolor la funesta melodía.

Note: By permission of the author.

Por eso a veces, reprimiendo el llanto,
cuando todo en mi vida se derrumba
de un acerbo dolor en los excesos,
me voy al silencioso camposanto
y dejo, entre tus flores en la tumba,
mi rosario de lágrimas y besos.

MOTHER OF MINE!

A token of my love for you
    sings the voice of my heart this day.
Heaven's light shines brighter
    when your forehead I kiss, Mother dear.

What else could I ask for? My happiness is so great.
    There's nothing comparable to my joy.
Because you are here with me, blessed Mother
    and your arms still embrace me.

Your pious, motherly caresses
    heal my wounds; you wish
For thorns not to cause my soles to bleed
    even though I run through the thistles.

You, who can foretell my dreams;
Mother, fountain of love, blessed are you.

ON THE ANNIVERSARY OF HER DEATH (1940)

Now that you are no longer with me, beloved Mother,
    In my home there are no more songs of joy;
And my suffering increases
    When I, in vain, seek you, blessed Mother.

Because far from you, my troubles are so many
    they impose upon me lethal melancholy,
And my lyre turned to dust, sorrowfully sings
    a sad melody.

That's why sometimes in suppressing my grief
  everything in my life is dimmed
Because of excessive pain.
  I go to the quiet cemetery
And leave among the flowers upon your tomb
  a rosary of tears and kisses.

Esperanza Montoya Padilla

🖋

MY NAME IS ESPERANZA MONTOYA PADILLA. I was born in Mascot, Arizona, on August 28, 1915. Mascot was a mining town in the Chiricahua Mountains above Dos Cabezas, which is near Willcox. My mother's name was Dolores López Montoya; she came from a small town called Huepac close to Cananea, Sonora, Mexico. I believe that her mother must have had a restaurant or boarding house in that town. The way my mother explained it was that my father, Quirino Montoya, and his friends Sam Shaw, Miles Standish, and Mr. Cockerham ate at my grandmother's place. That's how my parents met. My father was from Santa Fe, New Mexico. I think my dad married my mother in Mexico and brought her over here. I believe that she was about fourteen years old.

My father had a brother living in Willcox. His name was Juan Montoya. He also had another brother from Santa Fe named Lorenzo. We used to travel from Mascot to Alamogordo—I had two sisters living there. My mother was a midwife. When we went to Alamogordo to help with the childbirths, we stopped in Willcox and visited my dad's brothers.

My mother had a sister in Tucson named Josefa Molina; she was married to Francisco Molina. They were the parents of the Molinas who started the restaurant business. I remember my mother visiting her sister at their ranch out in Sabino after my father passed away. My dad died in Alamogordo, New Mexico, when I was nine years old. My mother died in Superior, Arizona, in 1941.

My parents had quite a large family. They raised thirteen children. There were my brothers—Manuel, Juan, Vicente, Henry, Eduardo, and Lalo, who was the youngest boy. My sisters were Sarah, Josefa, Felipa, Concha, Lola, Lupe, and Barbarita. I was the youngest girl. Manuel was the oldest—born in 1880. He always seemed more like a second father to me than a brother. All of us were born in Mascot except Manuel and Sarah. They were born in the Bisbee area. I remember Mother saying that they had a boarding house in Tombstone during the commotion of Wyatt Earp's time. My mother and father moved up to Mascot in the

*Don Quirino Montoya, father of
Esperanza Montoya, with his
youngest son, Eduardo, in Mascot,
Arizona, ca. 1920.*

early days. My mother remembered when the Apache Indians
and the soldiers from Fort Bowie would go past our house. My
mother would tell us also the story of how my dad brought the
mail on horseback from Willcox to Mascot. He was like a one-
man pony express.

In the early days, when I was a young child, Mascot was very
built up; it was booming. It was also a beautiful place. There were
a lot of cottonwood and oak trees on the road going up toward
the mine and streams coming down the mountain. The school
was on that road, along with a grocery store and even a pool hall.
There was a confectionery in the pool hall where they sold goodies like ice cream and candy. There was a community center up
on the hill where they showed movies. I remember silent movies
with Rudolph Valentino. Even the people from Dos Cabezas
came up to Mascot for the movies. At Christmas they put up a
tree in the community center, and all the children in town would

Sarah Montoya, Dolores López Montoya, and Esperanza in Globe,
Arizona, ca. 1930.

get their Christmas presents. There was a road coming up from
Dos Cabezas to Mascot and all kinds of houses along that road all
the way up to the mine. Our house was on that road. I remember
a time when everything was *caballos*—horses pulling wagons.
The cars came later, of course.

My dad worked as a watchman for the mining company in
Mascot. At that time they didn't have banks around, so they had
to have a watchman for whatever they had of value, like the pay-
roll. There were mining company offices in Mascot. I guess there
were no local women who could do the jobs so they brought
them from New York. They were all nice-looking girls, well
dressed. They built living quarters for them, dormitories with
bathrooms and bedrooms and a big dining room. They had their
own cook. Roberto Paco was a carpenter in Mascot. He helped
build the dormitories for those women. Further up the hill in
Mascot was mostly the Anglo part. It was a big community.

The Black Cat was a special railroad car between Dos Cabezas
and the train station in Willcox. A limousine taxi brought the

mining officials from Dos Cabezas to Mascot for meetings. The only big shot who actually lived in Mascot was Mr. Prout, the superintendent of the mine. He and his wife had a beautiful home at the top of the hill; it had electricity and indoor plumbing. It had a dining room where they entertained the big shots from back east. My sister Lupe cleaned and cooked for them. She had a *casita* next to the entrance to the Prout's house. Those were her sleeping quarters but she ate in the big house.

Dos Cabezas was the part where most of the Mexicanos lived. That's where the "party machine" was. They had all the *fiestas Mexicanas*—*el Cinco de Mayo* or *Diesiseís de Septiembre*. There was a salon where they put on dances and celebrated weddings. There was music and dancing—very happy times. The musicians came from Douglas and Benson. In fact, one of my sisters, Sarah, married a man named Severo Palma. He was a smart man, an educated man. He was from Mexico, and he is the one who used to put on all these fiestas.

The two older sisters that I remember at home were Lupe and Barbarita. Barbarita was the one who used to take care of me. She saw that I was washed and combed and dressed and had my shoes and socks on. That's the way it was at the house. Everyone was in charge of someone. My mother used to chaperone them to the dances in Dos Cabezas because my father would not allow them to go alone. I had a brother-in-law named Nacho Pacheco who, even after my sister Josefa had died in childbirth, stayed very close to the family. He kept coming to the family as a son and called my parents Mom and Dad. I remember Lupe saying, "Oh! If only Nacho would come and take us to the dance! Because if he doesn't come, we won't be able to go!" My mother had a home altar—I don't know where this belief came from— but Lupe put the saints on my mother's altar upside down! She would say, "If you don't grant me my wish to go to the dance, I'm not going to turn you right side up again!"

So Mr. Pacheco would come to mother and say, "Get ready and get the girls ready. I am going to pick you up, and we're going to the dance." And my dad would say to Mr. Pacheco, "Here you come, stirring up trouble." He was very fussy; he didn't like that kind of stuff. My dad would say to my mother, "Are you going to take the girls to the dance?" And Mother would say, "Well, yes." "¡Pues si vas a llevar al baile a estas andariegas, tienes que llevar a todos!" ("Well, if you're going to take these gadabouts to the dance, you have to take them all!") So Mother would take me and my little brother Lalo to the dance with her, and there we were, leaning on Mother. We'd go to sleep on her lap!

The funny thing is, I remember these things and I thought that they were dreams of mine. And I'd say to myself, "Did that place have a balcony?" But yes! It *did* have a balcony! I remember a woman named Sofia Martinez—she was Nacho Pacheco's sister. She used to make tamales and menudo and she'd take it to the dance hall to sell and serve it up there on that little balcony. She was widowed and left with a large family and she struggled—like all women—and made food to sell.

I remember a man at the dances whose name was Macario Ortiz; he was a character. They used to say, "Aquí viene Macario. Los viejos esconden a las viejas y las madres a las hijas." ("Here comes Macario. Husbands hide your wives, and mothers, your daughters.") He'd come and bring all the latest dances and all the latest fashions. He was so good looking and always "duded up" in riding britches. There was a song about the dandies of Dos Cabezas with their balloon pants and their celluloid collars. I think Macario made up that song. They used to sing it at the dances! He used to sing and play the guitar; he was always welcome!

CANCIÓN	SONG
Los tipos de Dos Cabezas	The dandies of Dos Cabezas
Usan camisas de seda	Wear shirts of silk
Con cuellos de sololoi	With collars of celluloid
Y pantalones "balloon"	And balloon pants
Pero los traen enfiados	But they bought them on credit
En la tienda de Macaboy	At the Macoboy Store.

I don't remember him ever doing any work. I think he was involved in bootlegging and he was always in trouble with the police, but he was never afraid of anybody. Once when we were leaving the dance, I was holding on to Mother's hand. Macario was tied to a lamppost. He had gotten into some kind of trouble, and since there were no police in Dos Cabezas they had tied him to the lamppost until the police came in from Willcox. I remember he said to us, "Hermanitas, take me from here. If you're my friends you'll untie me!"

As long as I can remember, my mother always had a boarding house. In the very early days in Mascot, before my father passed away, there was a mine across the road from our house. The name of the mine was the Dives. My brother-in-law Luis Verdugo, Felipa's first husband, was killed in that mine. All the men that worked there used to come and eat at our house because there was no other place for them to eat in Mascot. In those years the miners did not sleep at our house. There was another house across from our home that was our property, too, and that's where the miners slept. It was a nice house with big wood-burning heaters and stoves where they made their coffee. Across the road, also, was a well that belonged to us. My dad was always very fussy about that well. When cars arrived up the hill from Dos Cabezas the drivers had to get permission from my dad to use the well to get water. Later on he put a lock on the well because the people were not taking care of it the way they should.

The boarding house was always part of our home. There were trees all around—fruit trees, mostly. Apricot and peach. My mother made jam. There were *trincheras* (rock retaining walls) that my father had built. The door that was the entrance to the kitchen faced the road that went between Dos Cabezas and Mascot. On the other side of the kitchen was a dining room, and a hall to one side of the kitchen where the miners washed their hands to get ready for dinner. At the entrance to the hall there was a chiffonnier with a pitcher and bowl and two little doors on the bottom where the towels were hung. One of my jobs was to go and check and make sure that there were fresh towels hanging there. On the other side of the hall was a room like a pantry; it was very dark and cool in that room, and that is where they kept the *carne seca* and *carne adobada*. There was a porch on the side of the house that faced the road, and the living room and our bedrooms were on the other side of the house. All of the windows of the bedrooms were completely covered with ivy so thick that you couldn't see in or out. I always figured that my dad planted that ivy so that no one could look inside.

Towards the road there was a fence all around that I used to hang on to watch the people go by. My dad had made some little steps out of rock. When I was a little girl, I used to sit there and wait for the men to come back from work to see if they had brought me a treat. Manuel Miranda, who married my sister Sarah, used to tell me, "When we'd see you, we'd say, 'There she is. Let's tease her. Oh, how are you? How's my girlfriend?'" I would really get upset. I wanted everyone to respect me. "Don't you be calling me your girlfriend! I'm not your girlfriend! I'm not a *novia* to *surumatos* (hicks)! You just wait! I'm going to tell my dad all these things that you're saying to me, and he is going to come and beat you up!" They used to get a big kick out of that. I was always complaining to my dad; he was very special to me. I thought he was the greatest.

Of course, my parents were very strict. They didn't want my older sisters to mingle with the boarders. When I was small, if they saw one of my sisters talking to one of the men, they would say to me, "Go and tell Barbarita to go and check and see if the hens are laying!"

They had a garden—they grew tomatoes and chile and a few other things. And of course we had our fruit trees. But one of my brothers, Juan, had a farm in Bowie, and he used to bring a lot of produce—corn, chile verde, sartas of chile, watermelons, melons—up to Mascot for our boarding house.

And they had animals, of course. My dad had goats, and he sold the wool. He kept a cow for fresh milk, and goats and pigs and chickens and even turkeys! He slaughtered so we would have fresh meat, and we had to have the chickens for the eggs, of course. My mother sold the chickens and turkeys, too. It was rare to have them; other people did not have these things. I think she used to sell the carne seca, too. She was always in business! Most of the slaughtering was done during the winter when it was time for tamales. When my father slaughtered a pig, my mother would make *carne adobada*. She made a sauce with red chile, garlic, onions, oregano, and other spices and then dipped the meat in the sauce and let it drain and dry. This is the way that the meat was preserved—there were no refrigerators in those days. I remember, also, that when an animal was slaughtered, they collected the blood, and they would take it to Mother in the kitchen. She put garlic and onion in it, and then she cooked it and stirred it until it thickened and curdled; it looked like chopped liver. They made *chicharrones* also. They cut up the pork skins outside and then cooked them in a kettle on an open fire. Everyone pitched in—there was a lot of action! The fat would be strained and collected in cans and saved. That is the lard that my mother used for cooking. I tell my kids that I love all those foods because I was raised with them.

My father was a perfectionist. He wanted everything orderly. He kept all the animals on top of a hill behind the house so that you couldn't smell them from the house. He wanted everything like that out of the way. And he made trincheras against the side of the hill so that the dirt wouldn't fall down into the patio. He also made stone walls by the road that ran by the house. It's not the boarders that count. It's those walls that my dad made. He was always working around the house and around the chicken coops—fixing them, cleaning them. He had some kind of tube for the pig pens—some kind of invention—where he could throw the food into the tube and not have to go into the pens.

Everybody had a job. We had big tinas that we filled with water so that the garden could be watered when my dad came home from work. We filled the tinas with water for the laundry and got the wood and made the fire for heating it. The boys fed and watered the animals. The patio had to be swept and cleaned. My dad was very fussy about the kerosene lamps; that was one of my jobs. I cleaned the chimneys. Wood had to be gathered for the stove and for the big wood-burning heaters. It snowed a lot in the winter, and it got very, very cold.

I tell my kids that my dad invented the frisbee! We used to have a record player, an old windup Victrola. But he didn't like all the music that was going around; he listened only to certain music, more classical I guess. The girls wanted to listen to songs like "Un Viejo Amor" or whatever was popular at that time. We used to laugh when Mother told this story. She said that when Dad wasn't around, they'd start the record player. They'd start in with the *bailadas* (dancing), and they weren't tending to their jobs! Everybody was having a ball, and Mother would say, "It's getting time for your dad to be getting home. You'd better check and see that everything is right." If he came in and they had a record playing that he didn't like, he wouldn't say anything; he'd just go out there and throw it up the hill! That's the kind of person he was!

My sisters helped my mother a lot—setting the table, washing and putting the dishes away, helping with the cooking. There must have been about ten men who ate there, but they would never all come at the same time because they had different shifts.

My mother had a lot of beautiful dishes. In those days there was no plastic. The dishes used to come in a great big barrel, and my mother would take orders for dishes from different women. For doing this she would get a set of dishes free—the little cream pitchers, the butter plates, the whole bit!

My mother had a great big wood-burning stove, and there was a big tank on one side that was used for heating the water. On the other side was a box for the wood. It had a pretty shelf for the salt and pepper shakers. The stove was set against a wall of solid rock. Our house was built against the hill, and my dad must have made that wall with dynamite. From the stove there was a step down to a big table against the other wall. That's where my mother did her cooking and baking. Under this table she kept great big cans of lard and flour. And there was another little table there where my dad used to sit and drink his coffee and look out the window.

My mother was a very good cook, and she could make almost

anything—American as well as Mexican-style food. She made a lot of *guisados* (stews) and caldos, and of course, tortillas. She had to make pies and cakes and cupcakes for the miners' lunches. She made puddings. Lemon pies were her specialty. Oh, how my brother Manuel was after her to make lemon pies—his favorite! She made the best *empanadas de calabaza* (pumpkin turnovers)! In fact, I still make them myself, but I wonder if I'm doing it the right way.

Mother would get up very early and put on the coffee and make breakfast and pack lunches for the men. She made fried eggs and potatoes. It was very rare that we would have ham, but she made her own chorizo. She also made pancakes and baking-powder biscuits in the mornings. And then, of course, she had to get an early start on the evening meal—caldos and guisados and tortillas or whatever. In the evening after dinners she baked bread and rolls. I guess that is when she had the time.

When it was Mother's rest time, she would sit down in her chair. I don't know what she was thinking. I was little—running around, jumping around—and she would say to me, "Abre el horno para ver como está el pan." ("Go open the oven door to see how the bread is doing.") And I would go and look and then go and tell her that it looked this way or that. My brother-in-law Cipriano Trillo used to say that Mother made the best bread! My kids always say, "My mother makes the best bread!" But I still think my mother's was better. Maybe it's because when you are a child everything your mother makes tastes so good.

She was never too busy or too tired to help me with my childish things. I used to gather walnuts, and with the patience of a child I would sit and crack the walnuts until I had a cupful. Then I'd tell my mother that I wanted to make candy. She'd tell me, "You put in so much sugar and so much of this and so much of that and stir and stir and then you add the walnuts." We'd make taffy and when people were visiting we'd have taffy pulls.

Mother was also a partera. Whatever babies were born in Mascot, she delivered them. The men came to the house and picked her up. "Ay, Doña Lolita, mi esposa está con dolores!" ("Ay, Doña Lolita, my wife is having pains!") And she would get up in the middle of the night and go wherever she was needed. She never complained. We'd go to New Mexico to deliver my sisters' babies. I always wondered how in the world she knew all this. I don't think she ever had any problems, thank God. I guess God was with her, because everything went right, and they would call her again for the next baby.

Poor Mother. I remember when I had my babies, I went by the book. Everything the book said, I did. And my mother would tell me to give the babies tea when they got sick, and I would say, "No, no, no! I don't want to start your medications!" And she would get upset with me and say, "How do you think that all of you were raised?" "Well, I'm going to bring mine up different," I would tell her. "I'm going to be the modern one!"

Anyone that needed help would come to her. If they were sick, or if their babies were sick, they came to her for advice. She gave them medicines and comforted them. She gave the babies teas *cuando estaban empachados* (when they had indigestion or colic). She had all kinds of little jars with herbs. In fact she used to buy the herbs from the Arab and Jewish merchants who came from Douglas and El Paso to sell their wares, all kinds of things from a truck. She was always *curando*.

Y sobaba. She also gave massages to everyone who was sick. She made this stuff that was so stinky from turpentine and I don't know what in the world! It smelled worse than Ben Gay. People had faith in her healing.

There was no such thing as a church in Mascot or in Dos Cabezas. That's why I say that to be a good person you don't have to go to church, because to me my mother was a good person. She never said anything bad about anybody. If there are saints in heaven, then she is one. She didn't have the time to *andar de comadre*—to be taking and bringing gossip. She would go to someone's house if she was asked. And that's the way she brought us up. The funny thing is I don't remember mother teaching us any prayers. All she taught me was work! The only thing that I remember that we did as kids—when we were going to bed—she made the sign of the cross on us. *Me agarraba la mano y me decía,* "Mira, hija, por la señal de la Santa Cruz." (She would take me by the hand and say to me, "Look, hija. In the name of the Holy Cross.") She would do that every night to us. I remember so well when I was a baby sleeping with my sister and having nightmares. I went to my mother's bed. I would be feeling for her, and I'd wake my dad up. My dad would say, "What's the matter? What do you want?" And I'd say, "I want my mother." "What do you want your mother for?" "I want her to make the sign of the cross on me." So she'd hold my hand and do that to me and that would give me a good feeling. And then I'd start getting off the bed very, very slowly hoping that they'd tell me that I could stay there. I knew what my mother would say, but I was worried about my dad. "Can't you find your way to your bed?" And I'd say, "Yes." So my mother would say, "Just lie down at the foot of the bed."

Whenever we finished eating we always said "Gracias a Dios." My brother Manuel wouldn't let us ever get off the table until we said, "Thanks be to God." He got that from my mother.

My mother's altar was in the entrance to her bedroom. It was built inside the wall, with the wall as a frame like a nicho. That's where she had all her saints. The one santo she prayed to the most was a big statue of María Santísima, and she was the one that was in the middle of all the little saints. Of course, she had flowers and little decorations that they put on altars. But María Santísima was the saint that was very important to her and us, too.

There was a man who used to come to the house and say, "¿Doña Lolita, Ud. cree en todos estos santos que tiene Ud. en su altar?" ("Doña Lolita, do you believe in all these saints that you have on your altar?") And my mother said, "Sí. Ellos me hacen a mí mis milagros." ("Yes, I do. They perform miracles for me.") And so it happened that this man got very sick, and he called for my mother and she went over to his house to see if there was anything she could do for him—pray with him, give him medicine or a massage. He said to her. "Doña Lolita, tell your saints that perform miracles for you if they won't grant me a miracle, too." Mother used to tell us, "Then he believed and had faith in the saints!"

When I was about seven years old, everything changed for us.

I think that somehow my dad knew that he was going to die, and he didn't want to die in Arizona. He wanted to go back to New Mexico. So Dad and Mother closed up our house in Mascot and left an old couple in charge of things. We went to stay with my sister Lola—she was married to José Chavez—because they had a big two-story house in Alamogordo. I had another sister, Concha, who also lived in New Mexico. She was married to Pete Preciado. They had an orchard in Bent, and they grew everything that you can think of—grapes, *membrillo* (quince), pears, pomegranates, sugarcane, watermelon. They used to make jams, and they had little stands where they sold the fruit and jam to the people who were traveling to Mescalero to go to the *fiestas de los Indios*. They traded with the Indians, who had beautiful blankets and baskets.

I don't remember exactly how long we stayed in New Mexico before and after the death of my father. You know how time is when you are a child; days seem like months, and months seem like years. But I don't think that it was more than a couple of years altogether. When my dad passed away, Alberto Sandoval—a nephew of his who had become widowed—wanted my mother to go and take care of his family. He had six or seven children. He said he would take care of us—she wouldn't have to worry about anything. We went and stayed there for a while, but my mother was not the type to be dependent and quiet. She wanted to go back to Mascot.

Those were the years when the mine began to go down. Most of my memories of the place are of when it had begun to come apart. In my dad's time there were only old-timers there—Mexican people from way back—from Bowie and Willcox. But later they started bringing *renganches* (bunches of people) from Mexico, and they didn't have any homes, so they started to put up tents. It was the first time in our lives we had seen people from Mexico. They brought them to work in the mines. My father had always been in control—he was a tough person—but my mother was very kindhearted. She started giving away more than she should have. There were always people asking her for money. "Que deme dinero. Que voy a traer a la familia." So they could bring their families. It was all right when things were going well, but when everything at the mine began to go down, we began to struggle. She didn't have any savings.

My mother didn't have time to wash when we were alone. She had a woman washing for her; in fact, that woman was killed by her husband. She lived not very far from us; I think they were newcomers there. They were living in a tentlike house. The woman was pregnant and separated from her husband. Lucía, her younger sister, was at the house at the time. She must have come over to bring the clothes. We heard the pistol shot. And then Lucía said, "It sounded like it was at our house." We ran over there. The woman had been washing clothes under a tree. Her husband was on horseback, and he had come over to make up with her or argue. But he shot her, and she fell right there where she had been washing. Poor thing. And the man shot himself, too, and he was lying there also. He had tied his horse to the tree. While all the commotion was going on, he got up on his horse and left. The murdered woman's mother showed up in the meantime and said, "I'm going to get him!" She must have been a bootlegger or something because she was always up in the mountains with the burros. She'd come down from the mountains with loads of wood—she was like a tomboy!

It was just the three of us—my mother, Eduardo, and me—when we came back from New Mexico and my mother started the boarding house again. The three of us shared one bedroom, and my mother made the living room into bedrooms for the boarders. That's when she started teaching me things. She taught me everything I know, because I used to help her. She'd get me up in the mornings so I could help her with the breakfasts and lunches. I helped her peel potatoes and make sandwiches. I'd make jelly sandwiches! Sometimes I didn't even go to school because she would say, "You cannot go to school today because you have to do this or do that." I'd go and order the food from the store, and they would deliver the things to her. I helped her make the *guisos*—I cut the onions and stirred while she was cutting the meat. I set the table and washed the dishes. And then I was always having to watch the oven. "Mira en el horno—como está el pan"—for whatever she was baking. My mother couldn't send me to school, but she gave me the greatest school in the world, how to be a good mother and take care of my children. She struggled so much, but she taught me the good things of life. She never thought of herself.

Neither Eduardo nor I ever finished a year of school anywhere that I remember. The older ones, yes, but after my father died we were forever on the road. We'd leave to go and help someone have a baby, or I'd have to stay home and help my mother with the work of the boarding house. Or she'd wake me up in the middle of the night to go and deliver a baby, and she'd say to me, "Mihijita, I'm leaving. You get up in the morning and make cereal or oatmeal. Get your brother up; wash his hands and face, dress him, and give him breakfast. Then put things away and clean the house."

To this day, I don't remember what happened, but the reason that we left Mascot for good was because someone was scaring us. I think someone wanted us to go so that they could go in the house and rob us. When we would go to bed—there were no lights there at night in Mascot—everything was *dark*. We had an oil lamp that Mother kept lit, and the three of us slept together in the same bed. The minute we'd go to bed someone would pull on the door toward the well—the same door every night. And remember the vines on the window? They were *thick*—had been there for years and years. We could hear them being pulled apart so someone could look in. Honest to God, that was one of the worst feelings of my life and my childhood. I never did say that I was scared—I must have learned that from my mother. We'd go to bed scared. I could see her preparing for bed. She had a bat and she used to put it by the bed. I don't ever remember her saying that she was afraid. This was home for her, but she didn't know that she was going to go through all this, that everything was going to die down and that Mascot would become a ghost town.

We were alone. Dos Cabezas was down below. The other houses were up above us by the mine. That's where the *puros Anglos* (Anglos of means) lived. They didn't want what we had. And whoever was pulling on our door could have opened it, right? *Why?* I remember Mother getting up the next day and going outside and checking, and I'd be walking around with her. But she never said, "Ay, I'm afraid. What are we going to do?" When my brother Manuel and Paula came in to visit, Mother said to him, "Mira. Esto está pasando todas las noches. Vienen y nos asustan." ("Look. This is happening every night. Someone comes and scares us.") And he said, "No. No los asustan. Son los espantos. Esta casa tan vieja y tantas cosas que han pasado aquí." ("No. No one is scaring you. It's ghosts. This is such an old house and so many things have happened here in the life of this house.") While my dad was still alive, Juan and Barbarita had died very young in the house. They died of tuberculosis and those were the ghosts that my brother was talking about.

That very night Manuel told Mother, "Ándale. Vámonos." We left the very next day. She just took the clothes for the three of us and left everything. She closed up the house and didn't leave anyone taking care of it. She couldn't take anything—that's how bad it was! This happened when I was about eleven or twelve years old.

After we left, whoever it was did a good job of robbing us. They took everything—dishes, jewelry, furniture, anything of value, even the santos. I remember that Mother had La Pasión de Jesucristo—Jesus on the cross with María and Magdalena and the apostles all around—figures of gold inside a glass case. They took that. We had all these portraits hanging on the walls. They stole the frames and threw the pictures down on the floor. Of course, that didn't only happen to us, it happened to a lot of people when the mine started to go down, when Mascot became a ghost town.

In fact, we went over to Mascot a few years ago, and the house is gone. There's nothing left. I saw my mother's stove thrown by the side of the road halfway down the hill. Some of the trincheras that my dad built are still there, but the house is gone. I found an old shovel that I saved. And the stone step that my dad had made was still there. I said to my daughter Dolores, "Mira, hija. Here is where I used to sit when I was a child to wait for my goodies." My daughter said to me recently, "Mother, we should go back there and take a picture before the little step is gone, too."

When we first left Mascot, we went to stay with Manuel and Paula and their family at La Bonita Ranch near Willcox. Manuel was working for Mr. Hooker as a cook; he would go on the roundups. Then we went to Globe to live with my sister Felipa. She and her husband had bought a house, but he had left her. She had five children—one by Verdugo, who got killed in the mine, and four by Martínez. Mother was like "Handy Andy." Whenever anyone was in need, then there'd go Mother. Felipa started working, and Mother took care of all the children. She was home with all her kids and Lalo and me. Then my sister passed away and left all those kids and that house. We had to move out of that house because the family sold it so they could divide it up. The family went with their grandmother, Doña Sofia Martínez.

There was a woman in Globe named Sra. Jesús Pacheco—she had baptized me. At that time she had a boarding house where all the wives and children of the deportees would go and stay until they could join their husbands. Around the boarding house she had some apartments, and she told Mother that we could move into one of those little apartments. So that's where we ended up.

By that time I was working. I had to work, although I was not of age. I must have been around fourteen at that time. I worked with an older English couple. He was a retired missionary. They had glass cabinets filled with ugly things that they had brought from Africa. I'd go to their house in the mornings and make them breakfast and make up their beds and clean the house and cook for them. They had this old dried-up fish that I soaked and fixed for them.

I did go to school for a while in Globe. I went to Central School and then to Hill Street School, but I never finished a whole year. Something always went wrong. One time the truant officer picked me up while I was working. He took me to the welfare, and the social worker took me to our house. I think that she expected to find the house and family dirty, but we were not raised like that. Everything was very clean and in order. So she decided that we didn't need any help after all.

By that time everyone was pitching in to support Mother. Sometimes my brother Lalo feels bad because we struggled so much, and I tell him, "Don't feel bad. Nobody ever gave you anything. We paid our own way all the time. Look at what you learned!" I guess he feels bad because we didn't have a house. We had to roam around, always at someone else's house. I tell him that we *did* have a house at one time, to remember the good things. He says, "I don't remember." And I say, "Too bad, because *I do*."

I got married when I was quite young, while we were living in Globe. My mother would stay with Concha or Lupe or Sarah or me. Even when she was older, my mother was a hard worker. After she had her stroke and her left arm and hand were paralyzed, she would do mending, make quilts out of scraps or little aprons or dish towels. My niece Julia Trillo remembers that Mother would ask her and her sister Gloria to stand by the sewing machine so they could thread the needle and pull the material this way and that way, and Mother could use her good right hand to turn the wheel. She never felt helpless, and she never complained.

My children used to play with her. She loved children hanging on to her—all my nieces and nephews and my own kids. I didn't like her to do work for me, but when I would go out she'd tell my kids, "Go get me some wood. I'm going to make you some *champurro* or *sopaipillas* or donuts or tortillas." Champurro is a drink made with cocoa and cinnamon and a little thickening. My children remember that.

I had four children by my first marriage to Marcos DeLeón—Marcos Jr., Bernice, Hugo, and Dolores. I worked all those years. One time I went to visit my brother Manuel and Paula when he was working at a guest ranch in Sonoita called La Hacienda de Los Encinos. He was the wrangler in charge of the livestock. I had three children by that time; they were babes. Manuel told me that they needed a cook at the guest ranch. I said, "I don't know if I can cook for all those big shots." "You can do it," he said. So I got the job, and I started cooking for them. The owners of the ranch were named Carr; Tapper was the name of the Americano who managed the ranch. They liked me, and later they put me in charge of the housekeepers. They had all these people from Mexico working there cleaning the rooms and waiting tables.

We lived in Phoenix during the war. I started working again. Goodyear had a factory where they made the parts of the planes. I used to drill and buck—make holes for the rivets on the planes. During the war you couldn't buy refrigerators or cars or washing machines or anything like that; they were saving for the war. But I had a washing machine. At that time we were living in a project called Alzona Park. There were a lot of Italian people from back East who lived there. They'd bring me bundles of clothes, and I used to do wet wash for them. There were no dryers in those days. Everything was hung out on the line to dry. That's why it was called wet wash. I even used to cut their hair. I had learned that from my mother, too! I worked the night shift at the factory and then I'd come home and clean the house and wash and take care of the kids and fix everything up, and then do the laundry for the Italianos. I went from one job to the other. If I didn't inherit my mother's ability to work!

Later on when we moved to Tucson, I got a job at the Chicken Castle on West Congress. When I started working there they had just chicken and steak, but I introduced Mexican food; I managed the Mexican food part. Then I got a job at the Milkprint inspecting the seal on the plastic bags for mixing the margarine. The seal had to be just so. It was a good-paying job, and it had benefits, but it was not very steady. We would make a certain number of bags, and then we would get laid off. I guess if we made too many it wouldn't last, maybe because of the heat or the little dye in the middle. After a while we'd be called again to work. But I had to have steady work, so I got a job at Georgette's Lunch Counter on North Sixth Avenue. I had the night shift at the Milkprint, and I'd go to Georgette's after leaving there in the morning. They used to have banquets for the stores during the holidays and meetings for certain clubs. They'd call me to go in the morning for the breakfast meetings. I remember making as many as 120 or more pies in one day during Christmas and Thanksgiving! I used to be so tired! At that time my two sons had

joined the Air Force. I was so sad and lonely that I would cry.
Georgette used to tell me, "Hope, you're going to make the pie
crust salty with all your tears!"

Later I went to work for the L and L Restaurant on South
Fourth Avenue. It was just a little shack when I started working
there. They had nothing but hamburgers and barbecue. After I
was there a short time I started making Mexican food. I made
them what they are today. I made gallons and gallons of beans
and chile con carne and chile verde and tacos and sauces—all
kinds of sauces. I used to have big arms. My back and arms were
full of muscles from so much stirring. Stirring and mashing
beans. I made them a lot of money. When I left, the owner said
to me, "Esperanza, write these things down for me." And I said,
"Oh no, I'm dumb enough to work for you, but I'm not dumb
enough to give you my recipes!"

By that time I had remarried. I have a son, Larry, from my second marriage. But I always worked. For a time we lived on Wood
Street in Barrio El Hoyo. I had a gas stove and was shocked to
learn there was no gas in that neighborhood. So I got a petition
and went around getting signatures from the women there and
the city finally put in gas! Later I bought a house on Tennessee
Street with my own struggles. My son made the house I'm living
in now for his mother-in-law, but she changed her mind about it.
So I sold the house on Tennessee and bought that one. Now that
I'm retired, my children have started showering me with all kinds
of goodies and gifts.

I thank God for my parents. I felt very close to my father. He
was very strong and proud. He built our house. He was always
working. All our lives changed after he died. My mother meant
so much to me; she gave and taught me things that have helped
me throughout my life. I feel very proud. I wouldn't know how
to do anything if it weren't for Mother. And to this day I can
cook anything; you tell me what to cook for you and I'll cook it.

I thank God that my children did well after the struggles I
went through. We are a close family. Now all the rewards are
coming to me. All my blessings are my children.

I have two kitchens and ramadas all over the place. I do my

heavy-duty cooking—bread and pies and menudo—on the porch. My kids tell me that I'm always thinking about food! I guess I inherited that from my mother. When we lived in Mascot, there were always people going and coming to the mine, and they would go by our house. Mother would always take out the *empanadas*, or the cookies and coffee. So, everybody that comes to our house, I fix them something to eat. I don't know what it is with me. I always have to be making food and goodies for my family.

Virginia Gastelum

MY NAME IS VIRGINIA GASTELUM. I was born on October 18, 1908, at Estación Llano, Sonora, Mexico. My father's name was Santiago Gastelum. He was born in Tubutama, Sonora, Mexico, in May 1866. Tubutama is in the Distrito de Altar. My father died in 1961, two months before his ninety-fifth birthday. My grandfather's name was Guadalupe Gastelum. He was born in Tubac, Arizona, in the early 1800s. He died there when he was very old, when my brother Carlos was a baby. My grandfather was first married to Rosario Rosales. She was the mother of my father. I have her picture. Beautiful lady. And dressed so beautiful. I'm very proud of her. That's why my younger sister was named Rosario.

After my father was born, my grandmother Rosario separated from my grandfather and went to California to live. She married again and had another family—three boys and a girl. My grandfather also married again—the second time to Margarita Ochoa. They had quite a large family. My father had ten half-brothers and sisters. Their names were Viviano, León, Guadalupe, José, Ignacio, Nicolás, Tomás, Librada, Ana María, and Manuela.

By that time my grandfather had gone to Mexico to live. I don't know why. Many years later my father brought the family back from Mexico. They came in wagons and on horseback. They brought the goats with them, too. They were all American citizens because my grandfather had been born in Tubac. My father brought them because he wanted them to have a place to live where their lives would be better. He wanted them to know about the land. So everyone signed for a piece of land; their names are in the records in the court in Nogales. The family built a house, and they settled in Tubac for many years. My grandfather had a goat ranch, but he got old and sick and couldn't walk, and so the sons had to take over. My grandfather Guadalupe is buried in Tubac. They still use the cemetery for the relatives; the funerals go all the way from Carrillo's in Tucson to Tubac, except for my father. We made him understand that all our family is supposed to be together in Tucson.

They sold the homestead and all the brothers and sisters

moved away. Some of their children have gone to Tubac to visit because they heard about the land, but everything has fallen into ruin. There is nothing left of the house anymore.

When my father was growing up in Mexico, his mother would write to him from California. My grandfather saved the letters and gave them to him to read. He told him, "When you are a man, I want you to go and meet your mother." So my father came from his birthplace in Sonora to Los Angeles to find his mother. He came to the Tanque Verde where the Campas lived. They were my father's uncles and cousins. He went there to leave his horses. He couldn't take them to Los Angeles. He sold one of them for the train fare.

My father's cousin Oriol Armenta went with him to the train station. It was too early for the train, and they went to sleep in the luggage carts. During the night, the train passed by and left them fast asleep, so they had to wait for the next train to Los Angeles.

When my father got to Los Angeles, he found a taxicab and told the driver, "Take me to this place." He went to the address in the letters. He got out of the taxicab and knocked on the door, and he found his mother. He used to tell us that story and he made us cry; he told the story exactly the same way to everybody. There are people who still remember him and the stories he told. Everybody admired the way he was—very frank, very free, talking with all his heart.

My father's mother died when he was working as a cowboy for the Oteros in the Baboquívari. He didn't get the telegram telling him to come until it was too late. Many, many years later, when he was already an old man, he worked for the Sanitation Department for the city. He worked sweeping the streets and sidewalks downtown around Broadway and Congress. There wasn't much traffic then. He worked after the parades and things. Sweeping, sweeping, sweeping. He had brooms and a cart with a can to put the trash in. One day a lady came to him dressed all in black, like people do when they are in mourning. She had a rosary around her neck. She took it off and put it over his head. She didn't say a word. He just bent his head so she could put it on him. Then she disappeared. He told that story to us. "That was my mother," he said, "who came to protect me from the dangers." I had the rosary for a long time, but he said to me before he died, "When I go to the funeral home—when they get me ready at Carrillo's—this is the last favor I will ask from you. Put my rosary on me." It was very old, a long rosary that went to his waist. I did that for him—crying. I put it over his head when he was in the coffin. In his heart he believed that that was his mother, because he never saw her again; but he always kept in touch with his sister and brothers.

When my father was young, he came from his hometown in Sonora to work for Sabino and Teófilo Otero. He worked for them many years, at Tubac and Soporí and all those little towns. They also had a cattle ranch in the Baboquívari. They bought cattle in Mexico and brought them here and then took them to the Baboquívari Mountains. From the Baboquívari they would take the cattle to Amado to ship them on the train. My father would say that when they came to town they bought Levi pants and never took them off until they came back into town. "When we took our Levi pants off, they could stand up by themselves," he said. He made us laugh with those stories.

My father's first two wives died in childbirth. His first wife was named Ramona Salcido. They called her "La Señora," even when she was a child, because she was very quiet, very grownup; she always played alone.

After Ramona died, he married Manuelita Tapia. They were married in the cathedral—the first one in La Placita. Manuelita lived only a year after they were married. She and a baby boy both died in childbirth, but my father always considered Manuelita's father as his father—"mi Padre Tapia," he called him. He lived with us when he was a very old man. He lived to be almost one hundred years old.

My mother's name was María del Carmen Trejo. She was born in 1881 on September 14, at Estación Llano. I remember that date—1881—because that is the year the train crossed the line. My mother died in 1965. She lived to be eighty-three years old.

My father met my mother in Magdalena during the time that

they call Las Fiestas (St. Francis' Feast Day, October 4). All the girls dressed up beautiful and went around the plaza in front of the church. They'd get together by the arm—a string of girls going around and around. So when my father saw my mother, he said to himself, "That's my girl!" But there was no way he could talk to her or say anything to her about loving her or that he wanted her for a wife. My mother was staying with her *madrina* (godmother) in Magdalena while the fiestas were going on. They were very strict, so my father had to wait until my mother went home to talk to her and her family. He was a *caballero* (gentleman). They were married in 1905, and they came the following week to live in Nogales.

After a short time they went to live in Patagonia. My father owned horses and wagons, and the bosses from the mines hired him to haul material—lumber and everything—from Nogales to the mines. There was a very steep road on the hills going to the mines. They had to have four horses and two mules. They called a team a *flete*, and my father was the *fletero*.

My father worked all around that area. My mother cried a lot because her family was so far away; she wanted to go and see them, but they couldn't afford to make the trip. She was away from home and crying all the time and making her life miserable. But there were a lot of people there in Patagonia, and so she got acquainted with some neighbors. She loved one family all her life—they made them *compadres* (godparents). After that she loved that little town of Patagonia because that's the first place she made friends. They say it's a beautiful place, but I've never been there. I wanted to go because my mother liked it, but I could never go.

When my mother got pregnant with her first baby, my father took her to the doctor in Nogales because his first two wives had died in childbirth. He said, "I don't want you to die; I want you to see the doctor." So my brothers Rafael and Carlos were born in Nogales. When Rafael was born, my mother's father and mother came to take care of them. When Carlos was born, María—my mother's older sister who was a widow—came and stayed with them. They would stay for forty days taking care of the mother and the baby. My mother was very healthy; she never had any trouble. My mother went to Mexico to have me, and that is why I was born at Estación Llano, Sonora. After they baptized me in Magdalena when I was about a month old, we came home on the train. That was the best transportation we had!

At one time my father had a cantina in Tubac. He and his brother Viviano—the second oldest boy next to him—also had a homestead, a little farm where they grew all kinds of vegetables. But one year my father got disappointed because of the grasshoppers. He broke branches off of the trees and bushes and gave everyone a branch to beat away and kill the grasshoppers. My mother's sister Guadalupe remembered that. But they couldn't get rid of the grasshoppers; they ate all the crops. So my father became discouraged and said, "No more farming for me. I will forget about farming." And he did—for a while. When my sister Rosario was a baby—she is next to me—we came to Tucson to live because my father wanted to put my brothers in school. I know Tubac and Amado and all around there; I have been visiting there. But I don't remember anything about the house or living there.

The next child my mother and father had was a little boy they named Guadalupe for my grandfather. He was born in a little brick house that my father rented over on Main Street in front of Holy Family Church. My father wanted to come to Tucson so he could put us in school. Then we moved to Barrio Anita. We lived in front of the school on the corner of Davis and Anita streets. On the corner was a Chinese grocery store. We went there for candy when we were little. Once when Guadalupe got lost, Mother said, "Go and look for Guadalupe." Rosario and I went to the schoolyard and he was sitting there eating berries from a tree. That's what stayed in my mind! Oh, those years! Beautiful!

After that we moved to a house in Barrio Libre. From there we would take a streetcar to visit my father's brother José and his sisters Ana María, Manuela, and Librada. They all lived in Barrio Anita. I loved for my aunts to come because they'd take me everywhere because I was the oldest. We called the streetcar "El Urbano." It went down Stone Avenue and Main and all around.

The Gastelum family, ca. 1912. Left to right, back row:
*Santiago, Virginia's brother; Don Santiago Gastelum, her
father; and Carmen Trejo Gastelum, her mother.* Front row:
Virginia, far right, *with siblings Rafael, Carlos, Rosario, and
Guadalupe.*

Main had the old rails for many years. Not long ago they took
them out. Oh, we had beautiful rides on that streetcar!

When we moved to Barrio Libre I went to Drachman School,
but before I went to school my mother taught me how to read
and write Spanish. She was so busy with all the children that she
didn't have time to write to her family in Mexico. So I learned to
write Spanish; I wrote the letters, and when they answered back
I read them to her because she was always busy cooking or washing or spanking the children. My mother didn't have much
school, but she had a cousin who married a very educated man,

and he told them, whenever they said something out of place, "Don't say it like that; say it like this. This is the correct word." He was their teacher after they left school.

I learned English in school, but I didn't go to school very long. I left to help my mother around the house and with the children, but I kept on learning by reading. I love to read—the books, the newspapers. Every morning we had the *Star* delivered to our house, and I read the news for my father. He wanted to know everything about politics, and he even used to get *La Prensa* from El Paso. He liked the news from Mexico; he liked to know about the president. He was mad with the president of Mexico—Porfirio Díaz—because he didn't put schools for children outside of the towns in the rural areas. My grandfather Guadalupe had to pay tuition for his family to go to school.

Oh, how my father loved horses! We grew up around horses. He always rented a house in town that had a yard for the horses. In Barrio Anita and in Barrio Libre he had a corral and a little barn for them. He always had the *carro*—a heavy, heavy wagon—and the horses. That was the only transportation and the only way he could work. That is how we came to live near Phoenix.

There was a man that wanted the flete to take his furniture from Tucson to a place near Tempe. When my father got there with the furniture, the man didn't have the money to pay him. My father had trusted him to pay him, so he went to his friends who lived around Mesa working in the cotton fields. They were the Garcías, and they were like family to him; they called him Tío Santiago. My brothers Rafael and Carlos were with my father. There was a lot of work for them over there; they went to work picking cotton. They stayed there for a while, but then my father came home for us. We were living in Barrio Libre at the time. My father came knocking on the door. My mother didn't expect him without the boys. Before opening the door she said, "Who are you?" "Santiago," he said. "And where's Rafael and Carlos?" "I didn't bring them. Open the door and I'll let you know about it." He had left them over there picking cotton while the boss was getting ready to pay him. My father said, "I've come to get you. I'm going to take you over there with the girls and Guadalupe and

Manuel." I was about ten years old. Manuel was a baby. We went walking behind my mother from Barrio Libre to the Depot House to get the train to go to Mesa, and she was carrying Manuel in her arms. When we returned I was already a señorita—about thirteen or fourteen years old.

So we all moved to Mesa and picked cotton, too. But we didn't like doing that; we were not very good at it because we had had no experience. So my father went to the bosses, and he talked to them and got another job. We moved to another ranch, and he worked getting the pastures—the fields—ready for planting. Alfalfa and barley and all of that for the cattle. He raised turkeys as high as that table and took them from Gilbert to the markets in Mesa. We had a lot of turkey dinners, I'll tell you!

While we were living on that ranch in Gilbert, the family we were living with came down with the influenza. We had been living with them in a house—a very good house—but we had to move out and live in a tent. There were so many of us in our family that we had to have another wooden shack besides the tent. My mother was the cook; my mother was the nurse; my father was the doctor. They made the sick family sauco tea for the fever. None of us in our family got the influenza, not a headache, not a fever. We were camping in tents in the wintertime. We suffered a lot because it was so cold. My mother prayed day and night. God took care of us, thank the Lord.

Gilbert didn't have a Catholic church, so we had to go to church in Mesa. We traveled in a *carretela*—a wagon pulled by one or two horses. My mother worked very hard. She sewed for us; she made the boys shirts and our dresses and everything. And she cooked day and night. Sometimes she would cook our lunch and take it to the fields; she would fill up a ten-pound lard can with *gorditas* (small flour tortillas). She'd make gorditas all morning and *chile con carne* or *gallina con pipian* (chicken with pumpkin seed sauce). She'd go all the way to the fields carrying the food for everybody, with the boys helping her. So we'd have a great time—like a picnic!

My mother made the Sonora tortillas too—light, thin, big tortillas. Oh boy, there's nothing like it! I learned to make those tortillas from my mother. She made the best *masa*—the best dough! It didn't break. She used just lard and flour and water and a little bit of salt. No baking powder. I remember that she would always add the salt to the flour in the form of *la Santa Cruz* (the Holy Cross)—*para bendecir la masa* (to bless the dough). The Sonoran tortillas are made with milk by some people, but the tortillas are thicker and they don't stretch as well. It's better with water. You stretch the dough on your arm and pull it and pull it. We'd work them like that. I used to use my left hand, but now I can't stretch my fingers. My sister Rosario and I learned to make them on a *comal*; we always had a wood stove for the tortillas.

We had to go out of the house and do the wash in the water that was running in the ditches—the irrigation ditches. We helped Mother with the little children's clothes, but she always did the heavy part. She was very tall and strong; we didn't take after her in her height. Her arms were big and her hands were like mine—very big and strong. My mother got a tumor in her hand from that ranch in Gilbert, from working and washing on the board so much. My father had to take her to the doctor, and they opened the tumor and drained it. Her hand was never the same after that.

In 1920 my mother had to go to town so that she could have her next baby, and so my father rented a house in Mesa and we lived there for a while. But my little baby brother died; he wasn't very old, months only. His name was Gustavo. When my mother was in Mesa, we girls stayed with her and the boys stayed with my father to help him with the work on the farm. My father worked in Mesa, Gilbert, and Chandler. He planted alfalfa fields and watermelons and cantaloupes. He raised vegetables for the markets in Mesa. My brothers and sister and I even made the crates for shipping the cantaloupes to the market. Rosario was the champion of them all at making crates. She was small, but she liked to work. All of us children had to help our father because he was working on the farm and taking care of the animals.

As I said, my father always had a horse and wagon. My sister Rosario was a good driver, too. I didn't like to ride horses; I was afraid of everything, very timid. But not Rosario. She was like a boy—not afraid of anything!

The twins, Adán and Eva, were born in Gilbert. After that we came back to Tucson and my father went to work for Hilario Urquides at his farm on the Tanque Verde. We had a big adobe house with concrete floors. The farm was way east before crossing the bridge to Sabino Canyon Road. The Urquides didn't live out there, but they used to visit.

I didn't go to school again after the twins were born. I stayed home at the Urquides' farm to help my mother with the twins—they were very mischievous! I helped my mother with the cleaning, cooking, and washing. My sister Rosario went further in school, because my father had a cousin in town and she went to live with them so she could go to school. She went to Roskruge.

There were no cows or horses at that farm, just the land; but my father had his horses and a truck to haul the vegetables to the Chinese stores. He didn't have much school, but he was very intelligent and he read a lot. He knew when to plant because he had an almanac that guided him about the weather and when to plant each vegetable. He grew big, big onions. And fat, long ears of corn. And sweet potatoes and potatoes and chile and squash. Everything. He planted *frijol* for the house—for caldos and cocidos. He grew watermelons. When he planted the watermelons and saw a little one under the vines that were covering the ground, he counted the days and he knew when it would be ripe. And exactly on El Día de San Juan he would cut the first watermelon and go down the road and take it to his good friend Don Juan Valenzuela as a gift for his saint's day. Oh, yes, it was a very good piece of land that Urquides had there. Everything my father planted grew well.

Don Francisco and Josefa Molina, the Molinas from the restaurant, had the next ranch on this side before getting to the Urquides. They were farmers, too. They planted everything. That's where we started dancing because they used to have the fiestas for the saints' days! And they had musicians—guitar and accordion. It made good music for dancing. We used to celebrate saints' days instead of birthdays. Angelita Molina was a young girl, and we celebrated el Día de Los Angeles, August 2. María Molina's saint's day was August 15. It's a big fiesta, the Assumption of

Mary. Josefa Molina's was March 19, el Día de San José. The father and the son were both named Francisco and their saint's day was October 4. There was music and food, tamales and menudo. *Teswín* was the refreshment in the summer. My mother used to make it. She put so many gallons of water in a jar—those big heavy crocks. She toasted the corn—browned it in a pan—and then crushed it to break up the grains. She put so many cups of corn in the water and then added a dozen or so cups of *panocha* for the mixture of water and corn to start working. Then it was mixed with cinnamon and cloves. It had to ferment for a few days. And it was good! At the fiestas they had biscochuelos, and they'd take a tray and pass out the little cookies and glasses of tezwín to the people. The Molinas had a big house, and they would go from ranch to ranch inviting people to their fiestas. It was all Mexican people out there then.

When Adán and Eva got older, we moved into town so that they could go to school. That was in 1928. We rented a house on Convent from a lady named Sadie. She owned a store on the corner of Broadway and Meyer—La Casa de Piedra, my father used to call it. She was a foreigner, and she owned blocks and blocks of houses on Convent Street that she rented. For a while my father worked on a farm over by Cortaro where his brother José was a foreman. After that my father went to work for the city sweeping the streets.

While we were living on Convent Street in Barrio Libre, my father found a house to buy. He had a nephew—Nazario Gonzáles—who was a real estate person. My father told him, "Look for a house for me to buy. But remember, I don't have much money." So Nazario found a family who was selling a house at 431 S. Elias, and my father went to see it and liked it because it had a big yard. But we didn't have horses anymore. The time of horses was over. It was a good-sized house made of adobe. We needed a big house for all the family that we had. We had a wood stove for the tortillas. And we got a gas stove, too, when the gas came. And both of the stoves were working all the time! Our house was behind Carrillo School in what they call El Hoyo.

At the Gastelum home in Tucson ca. 1930 are Virginia
Gastelum, Otilia Maldonado, Rosario Gastelum, and Adela
Amado.

My mother had a beautiful garden at that house. She wasn't
too much for vegetables, but she loved flowers. We had lots and
lots of rose bushes. Those were her favorite flowers. We had dah-
lias. The seed is like a potato; you have to dig it and plant it. We
had a sidewalk from the front door to the gate, and along that
walk were *amamelias*, *lágrimas de María* (Mexican star lilies), tu-
lips, and lots of daisies—tiny little white flowers with a yellow
center. We had daffodils and lilies. We had trees, a lot of shade.
We had a *higuera* (fig tree) as big as a room. We even made jam
out of the figs. A beautiful tree! There was a grapevine growing
around a trellis, and in the shade of the trellis we had plants in
cans. My mother grew cilantro, *yerba buena* (mint), and oregano.

Those were the herbs we used for the food we made—the soups, like albóndigas. My mother had an herb called *álbacar* (sweet basil) that she had brought from Sonora, Mexico. I never see it anymore. It is boiled to make a tea for stomach trouble. If you touch a little leaf, it gives off a beautiful smell. "Ooh," you say! "It's álbacar!" It has a little flower and when the flower dries, there is a little stem with round, tiny seeds, a lot of seeds. Even the seeds have that beautiful smell! Plant them and they grow anywhere.

My family was always very religious. My mother had an altar in her room. She liked to pray at night with candlelight or just one light. When she was finished praying, she would put all her prayer books away in a little tin box. She had all the saints on that altar! El Corazón de Jesus (Sacred Heart of Jesus). Santa Teresita, San Antonio, La Virgen de Guadalupe. The Virgen de Guadalupe was a picture in a frame as big as that wall! My mother always liked her altar to be clean. She had little doilies embroidered and with lace. She washed them and even starched them and put them on clean all the time.

We prayed the novena to the Virgen de Guadalupe every year. My mother taught us that tradition. Every day we got together. Nine days of prayer—from December 4 to 12. And we'd stay awake all night on the vigil—the eleventh—to *amanecer* (greet the dawn). We hung white sheets down the walls from the ceiling to the floor to make a little room just for the Virgin. We pinned flowers and little balls—like Christmas balls—all over. I used to climb ladders and stand on a table and sew them on with a needle and thread. We had lots of flowers, paper and plastic. And sometimes we had the fresh flowers, too, for La Virgen. We must have roses for the Virgin. Roses are her favorite flower, as you can see in her picture.

We didn't have the money to go to Catholic schools. We always went to public schools, but we learned to pray at home. My mother was a good teacher; she taught those traditions for the Virgen de Guadalupe and the Santo Niño, too. We prayed a nine-day novena to him, too.

For the velación of La Virgen de Guadalupe, we said the rosary, said prayers, and sang *alabanzas* (songs of praise). Lots and lots of alabanzas and prayers. Books and books. We had a notebook that we used for the velación. We stayed up all night, as I told you, for the *víspera*. All night long we had to have the *lámparas* (oil lamps) lit for praying and singing. I washed and dried the chimneys and put the lámparas on the altar. I'll never forget it. "La Virtuosa Nube" is an alabanza we sang for La Virgen de Guadalupe. I'm going to sing it for you.

EN UNA VIRTUOSA NUBE

En una virtuosa nube me causó mucha alegría
Y en un arco de colores vi a la Virgen María
Coro: Se repite después
de todos los versos

Juan Diego quedó elevado de tan linda que la veía
Se acercó y subió a la cuesta a ver lo que quería.

"Hijo Juan Diego," le dijo, "una merced me has de hacer.
A Méjico has de bajar y al Arzobispo has de ver."

Tomó el Indio la calzada, luego a la ciudad bajó.
Entró en casa del Arzobispo y su embajada le dió.

El Arzobispo responde, "No sé como pueda ser.
Si una seña no me traes, hijo, no te puedo creer."

Triste se volvió Juan Diego a donde la Virgen le habló.
"El Arzobispo, Señora, una seña me pidió.

"Como me vió en este traje, mis palabras no entendió.
¿Por qué no envías españoles, hijos de tu protección?"

"Muchos tengo que me sirvan," dijo la Virgen inmensa,
"Pero mi gusto es que tu me hagas esta diligencia."

Como Reina de los Cielos, con sus manos poderosas,
Cortó y de señas le envió al Arzobispo unas rosas.

Se las echó en el ayate luego a la ciudad bajó
Entró en casa del Arzobispo: "Señas te traigo, Señor."

El Arzobispo responde que en la mesa las echara
Y en el ayate dichoso la Virgen quedó estampada

A sus pies se arrodilló diciendo de esta manera,
"Seáis bienvenida, Señora, para amparo y medianera.

"Señora, yo fuí el culpable que señas te pedí,
Dudando que vuestra alteza me viniera a ver a mí."

En fin, divina Señora, de rodillas por el suelo
Que todos los que te han oído los corones en el cielo.

ON A VIRTUOUS CLOUD

A holy cloud brought me much happiness
When I saw the Virgin Mary standing on a rainbow.

> (Chorus is repeated
> after each verse)

Juan Diego was transported at the beautiful sight.
He went closer and climbed the hill to find out her wishes.

"My son, Juan Diego," she told him,
"Go to Mexico (City) and call on the archbishop."

The Indian Juan Diego took to the path and went down into
the city.
He entered the home of the archbishop and gave him the
message.

The archbishop responded, "This cannot be.
If you do not bring me a sign, my son, I cannot believe
you."

Sadly, Juan Diego returned to the place where the Virgin had
spoken.
"The archbishop, My Lady, has asked me for a sign.

When he saw my humble garb, he did not believe my words.
Why don't you send Spaniards who are under the mantle of
your protection?"

"Many already are in my service," said the most powerful
Virgin,
"But I have chosen you to perform this errand for me."

And then the Queen of Heaven, with her powerful hands
Cut some roses and sent them to the archbishop as a sign.

Juan Diego put them in his mantle and went down into the
city.
He entered the archbishop's house: "My Lord, I have
brought you a sign."

The archbishop told Juan Diego to put the roses on the table;
And on the blessed mantle he saw the image of the Blessed
Virgin.

He fell to his knees and said,
"Welcome, my Lady, as a protectoress and intercessor.

"My Lady, I was at fault for asking you for a sign,
Doubting that Your Highness would come to one such as I.

"And now, Oh Divine Lady, on my knees I implore you
That all who hear you and believe, be crowned in heaven."

A holy cloud brought me much happiness
When I saw the Virgin Mary standing on a rainbow.

There is another song that they used to sing in Sonora where
I was born. For the novena, the prayers were always the same,
but the alabanzas were sometimes different. I remember one
verse of that song. I'll sing it for you.

Tu, que la fe trajiste a nuestro suelo
Querida Madre de la patria mía
Calma, Señora, nuestro amargo duelo

Si nos amas como hijos todavía;
Y recordando que dejaste al cielo
Por México infeliz
O, Dulce María,
Hoy que esté despreciado y moribundo,
Haz que reine ey lo respete el mundo.

You, who brought the faith to our land,
You, Oh Dear Mother of our country,
Calm our bitter pain
If you still love us as your sons.
Remembering that you left heaven
For our unhappy country,
Oh, Sweet Mary,
Now that it is scorned and dying
Grant that the world may respect us again.

¿Qué bonita, no? Muy bonita. ¡Para tenerlo en un record player!
(Isn't that pretty? Pretty enough to play on a record player!)

The last night of the novena—on the víspera—there was a supper for people who came. Two or three tables for the family. If other relatives and friends came from the neighborhood, we had to have extra tables. But there was always food for everybody. It was a very good fiesta that we had for the Virgen de Guadalupe!

We always made tamales. But my mother was a very good cook and sometimes she liked to make something else, like chicken or Spanish rice. She was an expert in making the *pipián de gallina con chile*. First you prepare the chile, grind it, sieve it, cook it. Then you peel pumpkin seeds and brown them a little and then grind them and add them to the cooked chicken and chile. *¡Qué bueno, qué sabroso!* (How delicious!)

The girls still follow that tradition. They start in one house and pray each night in a different house. They do it at night after work, because they don't have time during the day. They give everybody—even the children—a rosary, and they pray the rosary and the novena every night for nine nights. This year they copied the novena from Mother's prayer book, one for each family. It's an old, old book. I keep it in a plastic bag and bundle it together because it's coming apart. And songs—we had a book of songs. Now they have recorded alabanzas, and they play that during the night. The children love them.

There is a girl who comes here to visit me. Her name is Teresa—Tessie, we call her. She is from the Maldonado family; they were next-door neighbors on Calle Samaniego. Her husband's name is Jesús Juárez. He is a Eucharistic minister here at Devon Gables, and they come on Saturdays to give the communions, and she just comes to visit and talk to me about that time when she was a little girl and they went to the house to see the Virgin. She remembers everything. "What did you do, Ninny (all my friends and my nieces call me Ninny) with all the things that you had all over the ceiling and the altar for the Virgin? Where's the Virgin?" "Well," I tell her, "It's over there, with my things in my room at Amanda's house." After my sister Rosario died, I went to live with the youngest of the girls. I have a picture, too, of that altar.

We had some *tías* who were so very religious. They were first cousins of my mother. They were from Sonora. They rented a house on Convent Street by Drachman School. No matter where they lived, they always had the vigil for the Baby Jesus. We would go there and sing to the Baby Jesus. They had the *Niño Dios* in a little cradle. We would rock him slowly, very slowly. We would pull the cradle with ribbons. Like a little swing. We all had a turn while they prayed the rosary and sang. *¡Unas alabanzas tan bonitas!* (Such beautiful songs of praise!)

One of the tías was very *escrupulosa* about the altar and the Baby. She would stay right there and watch over us to make sure that we did not pull the ribbons too hard and tumble the Baby Jesus out of His cradle!

On Christmas Eve my mother liked to make *buñuelos* (tortilla-like pastry dipped in caramel sauce). Big ones! She made the dough with flour and water and one egg. *"Con un huevo,"* decía. *"No más."* No lard and no salt. She made the syrup from the panocha. She boiled the panocha and cinnamon together very slowly so that it wouldn't thicken too much and so that the syrup would be clear. *Clarita, clarita.* Delicious. Carmelita, the oldest of my nieces, still makes them.

Oh, how everyone loved and respected my father! He was very formal and serious, a very Christian man. The neighbors used to come and kiss his forehead or his hand and kneel in front of him to receive his blessing. They called him "Padrino" (Godfather). And, oh! The stories he used to tell about his life, about his experiences and what he had read. There was an alleyway behind the yard of our house, and people would go by and talk to my father. He had a big, strong voice. He was so good with words—very frank, beautiful conversation. I'll not forget it! When one of the nephews wanted to get married, he would tell his father and his father would tell him to go and see Tío Santiago. And it would be my father who would go and ask for the girl's hand in marriage. He knew what to say and when to say it! And the parents would give permission.

My father worked for many years. He worked hard. They didn't retire young like they do now. He was seventy years old when he retired.

During the Depression years he worked for the government. "El Chárite" is what the Mexicans called it. But it wasn't charity, oh no. They worked and worked *hard*. They had to dig and dig and dig. They worked for food; at least we did not want for food! The government gave them food—frozen tongue and cans of corned beef. We'd mix the corned beef with fried potatoes. They'd call the men to work to make patios and ramadas in the parks out of cement and rock. They worked on those little benches and chairs, over there in Reid Park. Randolph Park they called it then. It lasted a long time, that Depression.

My father had an accident when he was working for El Chárite. Mr. Castro, a neighbor, was the foreman of all the men. One day he came with his pickup truck to pick up the workers, and my father sat in the back of the truck and fell and hurt his back. He had to come home. The doctor came to take care of him at home. He picked my father up from his bed like he was a little boy and carried him to his car and took him to his office for X rays. It wasn't broken, but it was twisted. The name of the doctor was Dr. Kroeger. He was a big, tall man—as tall as this place. That *barrio* over there is named Kroeger Lane after him.

I never married. I lived with my parents at 431 S. Elías and took care of them. When they were old, they were both blind until they got that operation, and I used to read to them.

I worked at St. Mary's Hospital for a short time as an aide. I did not have a degree. In those days you did not need a degree. They used to admire the way I made beds. They said it seemed as if I had trained to be a nurse.

People would hire me also to take care of viejitos and sick people in their homes. They said I had a lot of patience. The family of María Rojas hired me. She used to live over on Alameda. I'd spend the day with her. They'd pick me up in the morning and bring me home at night. She had had a stroke; she couldn't speak. I would make dinner for her and her housekeeper and give her massages with a little machine. In those days you didn't need a license. You just did it, that's all. Now you can't do that.

When any of my nieces was going to have a baby, they would send for me. They had confidence in me. I did everything for them—took care of them and the babies like a midwife. I have even gone to California to take care of one of my nieces. They sent me the plane fare, and I went to Los Angeles. I liked that because I got to travel and enjoy myself.

Now, whenever anyone gets married, they ask me to give the bendición like my father used to do. They took me to the wedding of my grand-niece Carmen Teresa, so I could bless her. I am her godmother; I confirmed her. That was in 1987, and that is the last time I went out.

After my parents died, I went to live with my sister Rosario. She was married to Miguel Amado. I had to leave our house at 431 S. Elías. I couldn't take much; my sister did not have a big house. I took only my clothes and a few personal possessions. I took the big framed picture of la Virgen de Guadalupe. Even after that I used to go out and work in houses, but not for very long. I began with the aches and pains of arthritis just like my

Grandfather Guadalupe. And so all these years I have been seeing the doctors and trying to get well, but there is nothing they can do. There is only waiting.

Our house on Elías Street burned down. I think somebody went in there and started a fire. We never rented the house; it was empty. We had beautiful pictures, framed pictures of my mother and my father. We had a lot of pictures hanging on the walls of the living room. Everything was still there—beds and everything. And everything burned.

A phone call woke me up early in the morning. "The firemen just finished putting out a fire at your house." They found a metal box, and they looked in it and it was my mother's prayer books. They were all there, in that tin box. Nothing burned. The water did not hurt them. They asked me if I wanted to have the box right away. I said, "No, some other day." But they came and knocked on the door and gave me the box with the prayer books. I still have them. I still pray in one of them. It is my only treasure.

Rosalía Salazar Whelan

M Y NAME IS ROSALÍA SALAZAR WHELAN. I was born on February 4, 1904, at my parents' home in Aravaipa Canyon. My father's name was Epimenio Salazar. He was born in Oposura, Sonora, Mexico. He was a full-blooded Opata Indian. He was very ancianito when he died, very frail and partially blind. I think he must have been almost one hundred years old. He had been blind for about five years—it was caused by cataracts—when he decided to look for a cure. He went to Phoenix, El Paso, and finally to California where my sisters Pastora and Lucia lived. The doctors operated on him there, and he finally regained part of his sight in one eye. He had had other operations, but he wouldn't take care of himself. There he'd be, newly operated on and out in the milpa cutting hay with a scythe. He'd come back into the house at midday all sweaty and want us to pour cool water from the well on his head. When he finally got some of his sight back, he sent for us to go to visit him in Aravaipa Canyon. My husband, Wilford, and I were living in the little mining town of Copper Creek at the time. My father sent for us because he said he was eager to see us as he hadn't laid eyes on us in five years!

When my father knew he was about to die, he went to California to say goodbye to Pastora and Lucía. Then he came to Yuma to say goodbye to me and my sister Aurelia. He told us he wanted to return to his home in El Cañón. He wasn't in any condition to travel on his own, so some friends put him on the train from Yuma to Willcox. My brother Guadalupe picked him up at the train station and brought him home. He died in Aravaipa Canyon in July 1942. He is buried in our family cemetery there.

My mother's name was Crespina López de Salazar. She was born at Estación Llano, Sonora, Mexico, in about 1873. She and one of her sisters—my Tía Carmen—came with their grandmother Refugia—Doña Cuca—to Arizona when they were very young children. They lived at "La Posta." That is what they called Ft. Grant in the olden days when it was an army post. My mother had light eyes, and she was very fair, very blonde. They

Rosalía's mother, Crespina López de Salazar, left, and two
sisters, Aurelia and Pastora, ca. 1915. The baby, Ernesto
Parra, is Pastora's son.

called her "La Güera." She died in 1924 at the age of fifty. She is
also buried in our cemetery in Aravaipa Canyon.

In Aravaipa Canyon there is a cemetery where everyone who
lived there at that time was buried, but our family cemetery is
separate. One time my mother and I went up on a little hill where
there was a flat place that the cattle had trampled. She said to me,
"Look. The day that I die, this is where I want to be buried." And
so I told my family, and that is where most of our family is
buried.

My father was working at La Posta when he met my mother.
They were married at La Bonita, which was the name of the
town by the army post. It was a good-sized town in those days.

My mother used to tell me that my father was about thirty-five years old and she was sixteen years old when they married. They had eight children, seven girls and one boy. My oldest sister, Pastora, was born at La Bonita on August 6, 1891. The rest of us were born in El Cañón where my father and mother had gone to homestead. There was Guadalupe (b. 1894), Aurelia (b. 1896), Refugia (b. 1899), Lucía (b. 1902), myself (b. 1904), Luisa (b. 1907), and lastly, Victoria (b. 1909). Of all my family, I am the only one still living.

After my father and mother were married they went and lived in Aravaipa Canyon, but my father had already been to El Cañón as a very young man, before anyone had settled there. In the olden days, children were not allowed to take part in adult conversations, but I remember him sitting around and telling his stories with his friends. I overheard his saying that he had gone to Aravaipa Canyon looking for work. He worked as a cowboy there with a man named John Dunlap long before he and my mother were married. I think that is when he claimed his land there. [Family sources set the date of Epimenio's arrival in Aravaipa Canyon as 1865.] My grandfather used to come from Sonora to visit my father. He told the story that they were living near a ranchería on the San Pedro River and the troops of soldiers came to rout the Apaches. He was fearful for their lives and had to leave the area because the soldiers did not know the difference between an Opata Indian and an Apache.

My father was one of the first people to settle in Aravaipa Canyon, but later there were other families too, mostly Mexicanos, old families that had been there for a long time. I remember los Moraga, los Vindiola, los Martínez, los Vásquez, los García, los Samaniego, los Quijada, los Rodriguez, and los Santa Cruz. Tía Carmen also lived in El Cañón, and our cousin Clara who was married to an Americano named Sanford. There were some Americanos too, but just a few. The Campbells, who owned the T-Rail Ranch, were good friends of ours. Los Kennedy, los Firths, los Dowdle. Little by little over the years many of the families sold their places and left; I don't know why. Some went to Safford, others to Willcox. Some ended up in Hayden and Winkleman looking for work.

My father had a cattle ranch in El Cañón and a farm. He had a lot of land there. He kept most of his cattle in another place down below the canyon, towards the mountains. They called it "El Campo de Caballos." Later the Anglos named it Horse Camp. In those days the land was not fenced; it was all open range. All the rancheros and vaqueros in the area would gather the cattle during roundup and there would be thousands of cattle together in one place. Then they would drive the cattle to Willcox and ship them from there. It took them four days to drive the cattle that far.

My brother Guadalupe used to take care of my father's cattle at El Campo de los Caballos. From the time he was very small my father taught him how to ride a horse. My mother used to tell me that when my father would lift him up on the saddle and send him off to bring in the horses, she'd see at a distance and he was so small that she could barely see him in the saddle. She'd think to herself, "¡Pobrecito mihijito!" ("My poor little son!") All of us girls also learned to saddle and ride a horse at a very early age. But in those days one didn't wear pants; we wore skirts and rode sidesaddle. We called the sidesaddle "el albordón."

We had quite a few horses as well as the cattle. We had quarter horses for working the cattle and another kind of horse for the *tiros*—the teams that pulled the wagons. My father had four teams of horses that he used for the wagons for the farm to haul wood, the harvest to the barn, the grain and hay for the animals, and to carry provisions from Willcox. I, and sometimes my sister Lucía, used to go with my father once a year to get supplies—the staples that we did not grow ourselves. It took two days to get to Safford and three days to get to Willcox. *Toditito el día en el sol.* (All the long day in the sun.) We camped by the side of the road. He bought flour, coffee, macaroni, rice. He used to buy the coffee in great big barrels; he liked to buy it green because he liked to roast it himself. He said that it had a different flavor, that it was better that way.

I remember once that someone came to our house and saw the room where my mother stored the flour and sugar and coffee,

*Epimenio Salazar, Rosalía's father, and
Guadalupe, her only brother, ca. 1898.*

and he said to her, "¡Adio, Doña Güera! ¿Va a abrir Ud. una
tienda?" ("Good Lord, Doña Güera. Are you going to open a
store?")

We also used the teams for the boguecito that we had—it was
a surrey with a fringed top. We'd use it to go visiting the neighbors or to get the mail or a few necessities at the store in Klon-
dyke. Earlier, when I was a child, there was another store out
there closer to the canyon owned by a woman named Mrs.
Chambers. It had just a few things—cloth and shoes, but it closed
many years ago when the people started to leave.

Besides the cattle and other animals—chickens and pigs and
dairy cows—my father had a big vegetable farm and a *huerta* (orchard). He grew everything there on our *finca* (farm), every kind
of vegetable that you can think of—corn, chile, tomatoes, onions, carrots, squash, turnips, beets, different kinds of frijol,
green beans, black-eyed peas, strawberries, watermelon, and

cantaloupe. He grew grain—wheat, hay, barley. In the huerta he had different kinds of fruit trees—apples, peaches, plums, apricots, cherries, membrillo, and pears, different kinds of pears.

My father grew the vegetables for our family and took them to sell in Florence. He didn't sell in El Cañón because all the other ranchitos there had their milpas, too. But once a year he'd go to sell produce in Florence. He would come back with dates and oranges and grapefruit from the farm at the other end of the canyon. He had a lot of good arable land there in El Cañón; it was good land, very clean and fertile. There were not many people living there then. Nothing had fallen on it from the sky like we have now. But the flood waters have carried away much of my father's *terreno* where he had his milpas.

I used to have a little doll that my mother's sister made for me out of rags, and it had a beautiful china face. It was in the family a long time. I guess I must have played with it. I don't remember playing much as a child, but I do remember working.

It may be true that my sisters and I worked harder than the daughters of our neighbors. My parents only had one son, and as my brother Guadalupe got married very young, we had to fill in and do the work of men. As the older ones got married, the younger ones took over. When I got married, my sisters Victoria and Lucía stayed with my father to help him on the ranch.

Sometimes when I am sitting around and talking about those days to my friends that are my age, they say they don't believe me, that it is not possible that women did such work! I tell them, "It is true! When you have to, you have to! What you're taught, you learn!" But sometimes I stop to think and remember, and I say to myself, "How did we do it?" I remember nights when we would go to bed, and I didn't know whether or not I'd be able to sleep from weariness.

From the time we were very young we had our chores—there is always so much work on a farm. When we were small, one of our jobs was to bring in kindling at night for the morning fire. We had to get up at 4:30 or 5:00, and who at that hour is going to go outside and gather kindling? We had to milk the cows before we went to school, and then we walked to school. It was a couple

Rosalía Salazar in Aravaipa Canyon, ca. 1920.

miles from our house over there by the T-Rail Ranch. We had a clock—do you know what that clock was? We'd hear my father make a sound—hrrumph, hrrumph, hrrumph. And we knew it was time to get up, because we had to take him his coffee to bed before we went outside to start on our chores. He was the boss all right. He was strong, he was serious, he was well respected. *No era renegado.* (He didn't yell or get mad.) He was strict and demanding, it is true. But we never really noticed it; we were used to it.

As we got older we had other jobs as well. We washed. We ironed. We worked in the milpa. We picked fruit and vegetables.

The Salazar family in Aravaipa Canyon, ca. 1918. The photograph was taken on the occasion of Guadalupe Salazar's leaving to serve in World War I. Back row, left to right: Guadalupe and wife, Teresa Moraga Salazar, holding baby Teresa; Rosalía; Lucía; Refugia; Aurelia; Epimenio, Rosalía's father; and Crespina López de Salazar, her mother; front row: Guillermo and Adolfo, sons of Guadalupe and Teresa; John, son of Refugia; Luisa; and Victoria.

We hoed. From the time we were about fourteen years old we helped with the plowing. We used a horse-drawn plow in those days; later we had iron plows. You have to hold the reins and guide the horse while he is pulling the plow. *Y eso era andar, y andar y andar.* (And that meant walking, walking, walking.)

Now see here. The orchard was not close to the house. It was down the canyon. When the fruit was ripe, we had to hitch a team of horses to the wagon and take it to the orchard. We climbed the trees with ladders to reach the fruit. We hung a bucket with a rope, and as we filled the bucket with fruit we'd lower it. Then the others below put the fruit in boxes or tubs and loaded it on the wagon. When you pick fruit you have to be very careful not to bruise it, because it will spoil. Sometimes we worked all day—

and why not? At times my father would take a load of fruit on the wagon and sell it at the different ranches this side of Willcox. Sometimes he lost a lot of fruit because it would spoil in the sun. We brought the fruit home and stored it in a room until it was processed. Some of the apples we wrapped in pages from a catalog and stored in wooden barrels, and we'd have fresh apples all winter. The rest we processed, either put up in jars or dried. We helped my mother make preserves—jams and jellies. She even made jelly out of the apple skins. Everyone helped until we were done, even if it meant leaving another job.

What we did not put up, we dried. My father made long tables outside out of wooden planks. We washed and dried the planks very, very well and then we'd put the apples on the tables to dry—¡muy parejitos, muy parejitos! (All in a row.) Then the next day we would turn them over so that they would dry on the other side. It was a lot of work, days and days of drying fruit.

Some of the other fruit like the peaches and apricots we dried as well. We'd string the fruit on a steel wire. We also dried a lot of chile. We'd roast it and peel it and hang it on a wire and cover it with cheesecloth to keep the flies off. We buried green tomatoes in the sand and used them as they ripened. We stored potatoes and carrots in burlap bags in the shade. And everything stayed fresh!

And oh! That orchard was large indeed! In Aravaipa Canyon, some of those old fruit trees from my father's *huerta* are still bearing fruit. My sister Victoria, who lived in El Cañón most of her life, was in charge of irrigating them; some of the old acequias still exist.

Of course, there in El Cañón, the people did not have to pay for water, because the river has a lot of water. Everyone in those days had their own dam that they used to divert the water to the acequias to water their milpas. Later on, when there were more people who settled in ranchitos down the canyon, they would ask to borrow water to irrigate. They'd use the water for three days, and that is how the people in El Cañón shared the water.

When my father slaughtered a beef, we made carne seca. He'd send us to that ranch where I told you he kept his cattle, El Campo de los Caballos. They'd send us to the *mesquitales* (mesquite groves) to make *el jerque*. I'm not sure why they sent us there; perhaps there were fewer flies. We'd hang the meat on thick wire and cover it with cheesecloth. My mother had a large wooden box, and it was full of carne seca. And that's a lot! A person doesn't understand unless they've made it themselves. A little bit costs you a lot of work. Nowadays, if you buy a little cup, it's very expensive. But I don't like to buy carne seca anyway, because I don't know how it was made.

Do you know what else my mother did with fresh meat? She fried it and rendered the fat and stored it in big cans. Then she'd put the cooked meat into the lard and it would harden. It was preserved that way. When we were ready to eat it, she'd simply remove the meat from the fat and warm it in the oven. It was ready for eating!

These were some of the things we did to preserve food. In those days there were no refrigerators like there are today. They'd make a wooden box with little feet and put screen around all four sides and on the top. It looked like a little house. Then they'd wrap it up in *guancochis* (burlap). Then on top of the box they'd put a large pan filled with water. It had holes in the bottom, and the water dripped very slowly down the sides of the burlap to keep it wet. That was the only way to keep things cool.

My mother worked very hard. It was enough work just with the large family that she had. She was always tending to the kitchen, not only to cook for our family but for the men that came to help my father. Guadalupe Redondo planted with my father; Juan Martínez was his helper. Naturally, she had a wood-burning stove. She was a very good cook. She made all kinds of caldos and guisos, and carne asada chile con carne and fried chicken and baked chicken and *gallina con chile*. She made cheese and quesadillas. Of course she made tortillas. And she made *pan de levadura* (yeast bread)—a whole tableful!

I remember especially her rice pudding. She made it in the oven in a big baking pan. She'd put the rice in the pan and mix it with milk and white sugar and cinnamon sticks and raisins. If you *had* raisins! She'd mix up the white of eggs and put it over the top, something like a meringue. She'd bake it in the oven with a low fire. If the fire was too hot, it would fall apart. And you'd better believe that she'd keep on checking on it and stirring it! If it needed more milk, she'd add it. She'd cook it until it was light brown, and it was so delicious. I've never been able to make it as good as she did. Maybe it was the fresh milk.

She also made casuela. It is a soup made with the carne seca. She'd rinse the jerky well and then *la machacaba* (pound it with a metate). Then she'd put it in the oven to roast it for a little while, being careful not to let it dry and harden. It can be eaten just like that or simmered with garlic, onion, and tomato. It is delicious and has a lot of flavor.

My mother made her tortillas medium sized. *¡Y muy parejitas, muy parejitas!* (Smooth and even!) She used to say, "You girls never learned to make tortillas the right way. Except for your oldest sister, Pastora. She makes them like I do." Sometimes she even made tortillas from the wheat we grew on the farm. We'd grind the flour ourselves on the metate.

You know, I get to thinking. I say to myself, "Todo se acaba." ("Everything comes to an end.") When you get older you don't do things the way you used to when you were young. My sisters and I used to make lots of tortillas, piles of them, because when you go out to work in the fields you don't have time to come in and make them at midday.

My mother sewed for us. She mended. She patched. She made us our underwear from manta cloth. And our blouses and skirts and housedresses. She had a treadle machine, and she ordered material from a catalog. She even bought our shoes that way. Every once in a great while she bought us a ready-made dress. When we needed a little better dress, Tía Carmen made it for us, but don't think for a minute that we had many clothes.

My father had a *dicho* (proverb). *Acuérdense que no es pecado ser pobre, pero ser dejados, ¡Ay Chivarras!* (Remember, it is not a sin to be poor, but to be dirty, heaven forbid!) My sisters and I had the chore of the washing and ironing. It was a lot with that big family. We washed twice a week. And all on the washboard. We gathered wood and made a big fire and hauled water. We boiled the clothes and then added more hot water and rinsed everything twice. There were so many clothes to hang that we even had to drape it over the branches of the mesquites. And then we used those heavy irons made out of cast iron. We'd put them on the wood stove to heat. My mother helped with folding and ironing the dish towels. We'd also wash and iron for some of the Americanas—wives of the ranchers who lived in El Cañón—to earn a little extra spending money. There were times when I would iron from seven o'clock in the morning until five o'clock in the afternoon. When it was cold, we'd find a spot of sun to warm our backs; and when it was hot, we'd look for a bit of shade to cool us.

There were other jobs on the ranch that required heavy work that only a man could do. One was the roundups and driving the cattle, and another was baling the hay. We girls helped load the hay on the wagons with pitchforks, but baling was a man's job. The hay was piled in a great big box, and a man was on top tamping it down. The baling machine, which is called an *horcina*, was at that time drawn by horses. It was dangerous work.

Another job that men did was clean the dams and acequias. When the river flooded, the acequias filled with debris and mud. It was heavy, dirty work with a shovel. They also detasseled and picked the corn. Because the corn plants are very tall, we couldn't reach them. But we helped wherever we *could* reach. After the corn was harvested, it was dried and stored. Whenever we had the chance to sit down, we would remove the kernels from the cob, little by little. *El negocio nunca se acaba.* (The work is never done.)

Speaking of the harvest, I was thinking the other day about when we harvested and threshed the beans. We'd gather the whole plant and pile it up in big piles with a pitchfork in an area of hard smooth ground called *la hera*. It was so hard that it looked like cement. There was a pole in the middle of this area, and they'd harness up three horses to the post. The horses went around and around and trampled the bean plants and the beanpods. Then everything would be winnowed and the leaves and pods would blow away in the wind. I used to ask myself, how is it that the *frijolitos* are not crushed and broken with all that trampling of horses? There was always a lot of clean and clear water in the river in Aravaipa Canyon. Besides the crops we planted, there were many plants that grew wild that we gathered and ate. *La verdolaga* (purslane), *el quelite, el choal, la petota* (all members of the spinach family). *La petota* grows almost anywhere. It grows here in Patagonia also. It is a large plant and has a rather large leaf. It grows close to the ground and spreads like a vine. One day my sister Victoria and I were going up to visit our cemetery, and she said to me, "Ay! The petotas are growing! This afternoon I'll come and gather them!" All of these greens are eaten the same way—steamed, with a little garlic, onion, and tomato.

Verro (watercress) also grew in great quantities in the river. We ate that raw, like a salad green. And *yerba buena* (mint). You know, if there is a lot of water and you plant some mint you have to dig it out by the shovelfuls. That's how thick it grows. *El ipazote* also grows abundantly in the acequias—like the yerba buena. It has a strong flavor. My father used to pick it and bring it home and put it in his beans for flavoring. Boiled as a tea, it is also good for stomachaches. We even ate the greens from the beets and turnips that we grew in the milpa. We didn't waste anything!

Another thing that the people in El Cañón used was the little fruit from the tápiro. My mother didn't make *atole* (gruel) *de tápiro,* but other people did. It was used as a refreshment; it was thick, slightly sweet. They'd cool it in the "icebox." It was very good. Sometimes they also made elderberry wine.

I don't want to forget about the bellotas. The Apache Indians used to come down from the San Carlos Reservation every summer during the bellota season. They'd stop at the house to visit my father. They called him "El Paisano"; they were very fond of him. Whole troops of them would come on horseback, and the minute they arrived they would go to the milpa to cut hay for their horses. They didn't have to ask permission. The Apache woman is the one who is in charge of the horses. They'd tether them on long ropes and then feed them. They'd also help themselves to the produce in the garden, especially the corn. How they loved the corn! They roasted it on the open fire.

Once an Apache Indian wanted a watermelon, and he told my sister Cuca (Refugia). She told him she'd give him a watermelon in exchange for some *bellotas*. He gave us just a handful. Cuca said, "No. It's too few!" The Indian pointed to the watermelon and said, "Agua. Agua." That the watermelon was nothing but water! My sister got mad. "Apaches, Apaches. Everywhere. *¡Son mas renegados!*" ("Always getting in the last word!")

My sister Victoria said that as the years went by the Apaches continued coming every year, but more to visit my father than for the bellotas.

They came the year he died, and when my sister told them that my father had died, they didn't stay. They got very sad and went away, never to return again.

My older children played with the Apache children during those times. It fascinated them that the Apaches spoke English and they didn't. The Apache children also played American games like Ring Around the Rosie, Run Sheep Run, and Hide and Go Seek. You see, they were already going to American schools and that's how they learned all that.

It seems as if in those days there was not so much sickness as there is now. I remember the doctor coming to El Cañón to see Doña Juana who used to get those terrible pains. But as for the other people that lived there, we cured ourselves with the herbs that we found growing in the canyon. I can hardly remember a doctor paying a call. If someone was sick, all the women would get together and keep a vigil; they'd bring food or any other thing you might need.

Once when we were living at the ranch, someone came to tell me that my husband, Wilford, had had an accident. A horse had escaped, and they had gone up into the sierra to capture it. Wilford's horse had stumbled and he had been thrown. They had brought him all that way off of the mountain. I don't know how they carried him. They had even brought his saddle! So I hitched the horses to the wagon and with my children Harvey and Margaret I went to get him. We put blankets in the wagon, and my sister gave my children some biscuits in a little tin bucket. We went down the canyon. I had to open gates and find my way. It got dark; I could hear the owls cry and the coyotes howl. When I got to where Wilford was lying by the river, he was unconscious. He had had a terrible fall—even his hat was all torn up! *¡Ay, Diosito!* I don't know how he lived. We brought him back to the house, and when we arrived the neighbors were all waiting with food and a fire and hot water. They kept a vigil with me all night. The next day we took him to the doctor's in Safford in the truck from the T-Rail Ranch. He regained consciousness the following day.

As I said, we used to treat ourselves with the plants and herbs that grew there. El ipazote, boiled into a tea, is good for stomachaches. We grew manzanilla in little tubs. Manzanilla and sauco are very good for stomach upsets also.

We used the bark of the mesquite—the white inside part—for a purgative. In those days we always had a metate handy. Poom! Poom! Poom! We'd pound it and put it in a jar with water. It was strained and given with salt. *¡Chispas! ¡Todito le sacaba a uno del cuerpo!* (Holy Fire! What a purge!)

Something else that we used for medicine for stomachaches and fevers was *hierba del indio* (goldenseal). The plant has a strange little leaf. We used the root; we picked it at a certain time of the year. It grows here in Patagonia, but since hardly anyone gathers it anymore, the plants have gotten too large. The root is soft and past its prime.

It was with hierba del indio that an Apache woman who lived in Aravaipa Canyon cured all my family of the influenza that was killing so many people. The year was 1918. We were all stricken. The woman's name was Doña Josefa Durán. I remember she'd come to minister to us early in the morning and be all wrapped up in a blanket. So many people died! Whole families! Doña Antonia Acosta had five children—a daughter, three sons, and a little baby of three months. Her husband died, and the only child that lived was Pancha. Every day you could hear the sound of someone digging a grave at the cemetery.

I only went to school to the eighth grade. We didn't speak any English, and the teachers were all Americanos, but somehow we made ourselves understood. We'd get up early in the morning to milk the cows, and then we'd walk to school. I quit after the eighth grade because the teacher was always late to open up the school for the afternoon session after lunch. He'd go off with some of the bigger boys and go swimming in the river and wouldn't come back. And there we'd be waiting and waiting. We'd see him on the other side on top of the hill having a great time. And why should I wait around? Remember, when we'd go home in the afternoon, it was not to play. We still had to do our chores. We had to go and get the dairy cows off the hills and bring them in to milk them! And on foot! The trustee came to our house and asked me why I had quit going to school, and that's exactly what I told him. Anyway, it was a hardship for my father when we were in school. He needed us for the business of the farm.

Our first house in El Cañón was a wooden house. Then my father hired some men to help him build a big house out of adobe. We called it *la casa grande*. It is still there.

La casa grande was also used as a *salón de baile* (dance hall) for the fiestas that we had in El Cañón. When there was a fiesta we took as many of our things out of the house as we could so people would have room for dancing. That was our main form of recreation. A group of musicians used to come to El Cañón from Safford. The band was called Los Chevarría. They played so beautifully! People came from all around—from Willcox, from Safford. And they'd ride up El Cañón on horseback from Hayden and Winkleman. It was the most direct route. We celebrated many different occasions—Christmas, New Year's, El Día de San José, El Día de San Juan, July 4, and September 16.

And what fiestas they were! We danced two or three nights until the dawn. The poor musicians could barely hold up, but at least there by the river there was a lot of shade and a lot of water.

They'd go there to rest or bathe and refresh themselves if they wished. They had to because at five or six in the afternoon the dancing would start all over again. Whole families would come from all the surrounding ranchitos, and they'd stay there also for two or three days. They didn't charge for the dances like they do nowadays. My father and a group of men paid for the musicians and everyone danced for free. Later my father enlarged la casa grande and added a kitchen at one end. My mother made dinners. She cooked and sold food to the people who came to the dances. She charged fifty cents a plate. My older sisters helped to serve. And she'd say to us girls, "When your partner invites you to eat, don't be shy and retiring! Bring them over so I can make a little money!" Well, now, if the bachelors didn't invite you to eat, you couldn't very well drag them over. But when they did invite me, I'd eat very little so they'd invite me again.

How I loved to dance! We used to dance "El Chotis," "La Varsoviana" (Put Your Little Foot), and "Las Cuadrillas" (reels; square dancing). Don Lauriano Moraga, who was the father of my brother's wife, Teresa Moraga, used to call the reels in Spanish. Instead of "Do-Si-Do" he'd call out, "Val En So!" I think we danced the cuadrillas a bit differently than the Americanos did.

The Moraga family was very musical. My sister-in-law played the guitar. My mother-in-law, Ignacia Whelan, also sang and played the accordion as well as the guitar. They sang the old-fashioned songs. One of my favorites was "Amor de Madre." Once in a while they play it on the Mexican radio station. I like it very much because it reminds me of my mother-in-law.

AMOR DE MADRE

Dame por Dios
Tu bendición
O Madre mía adorada

Que yo a tus pies
Pido perdón
Por lo que tanto has sufrido
A donde estás
En la mansión
Una mirada te pido
Madre querida
Ruega por mí al Creador.

Tu que estás en la mansión
De este reino celestial
Mándale a mi corazón
Un suspiro maternal;
Un suspiro maternal,
Un suspiro maternal,
Que me hiere, que me hiere
El corazón.

Mira, Madre, que en el mundo
Nadie te ama como yo
Mira que el amor de Madre
Es tan grande como Dios.

Mira, Madre, que en el mundo
Nadie te ama como yo
Se acabó el amor de Madre
Que era mi única ilusión.

A MOTHER'S LOVE

Bless me, in the name of God
Oh, my beloved Mother.
I kneel at your feet to ask forgiveness
For all that you have suffered.

I beg you to look down upon me
From the heavenly mansion
And I ask you to pray to God for me.

You who abide in the mansion
Of that celestial reign
Send to my heart a maternal sigh
For my heart is wounded.

You see, dearest Mother,
No one in the world loves you as I do.
You see, a mother's love is as great
As the love of God.

You see, Mother, no one in the world
Loves you as I do . . .
Mother's love is gone now,
It was my only hope and promise.

Don Lauriano's wife, Doña Juana Moraga, was the person who taught us our catechism. But I tell you, she was also one who was very enthusiastic about the music dances, too! Many, many years later, in the 1940s, my brother Guadalupe and my sisters Pastora and Victoria decided to make a capilla out of la casa grande in thanksgiving. It is the Salazar family chapel now. We have weddings and funerals there. The priest goes there to say mass. There are a lot of pretty saints in that chapel that a lot of señoras have brought. San Martín is there, and La Virgen. The Stations of the Cross. Pastora brought El Niño de Praga. Francisco (Pancho)—Victoria's son—brought El Sagrado Corazón that is by the door. My niece Cristina Pacheco and her husband, Alejandro, are the treasurers in charge of the chapel. Now, when they want to have a fiesta there, they just cover the saints with sheets. After all, Victoria used to say, "The saints love music too!" And she used to say, "A el que no le gusta la música, no tiene corazón." ("Anyone who doesn't like music, doesn't have a heart.")

In the olden days we were so isolated and the only way of travel was by a horse. People prayed on their own, the best they knew how. When the priest did come, the people offered their houses and fixed up a room with an altar. They'd hang sheets and put up Our Lord and the saints. One year the priest had not come to El Cañón for a long time. He was going to say a mass at the Whelan Ranch in the Sulphur Spring Valley, and my father-in-law-to-be, William Whelan, said that we'd better go, because there were a lot of children in El Cañón that had not yet been baptized. I went to the Whelan Ranch to baptize a nephew. A lot of other women went as well. That is how I met my husband Wilford. We were married in 1923, and that is the first time I had ever left El Cañón.

My mother died before our first child, Margaret, was born. We were living at the 76 Ranch and I was expecting, and Mother came to stay with me. I remember so well the morning that she died. We had been cleaning up around the house and yard and we were going to throw the trash into an empty windmill tank. We decided to wait until the next day because it was so windy. It was the month of March. I had put the tub down with the trash, and when I looked up I saw that Mother was falling. She had grabbed on to the wire fence. I got very scared and I said, "Mother! What's the matter? Speak to me!" There was no one to shout to for help! So I lay her down, and I took off running to the ranch house headquarters. It was a mile and a half and I ran all the way, as pregnant as I was. I found Howard the cook there and told him that my mother had fallen and I needed help. He went outside to call the cowboys who were butchering. By the time I went out the door Tomás was already getting on his horse. I followed him, running all the while. By the time I reached the well in the field, I could see that he had picked my mother up and was carrying her up the steps into the house. He lay her down in bed. By the time I arrived she was not responding. A nice black woman who knew a little doctoring came and started to make her a mustard plaster or something, but then she turned to me and said, "She's gone."

Válgame, Dios. (Oh Good Lord.) I didn't know what to do. My husband Wilford was gone far away in the Rincon Mountains. My compadre Julian Acevedo came by to see how Mother was doing. "No," I told him. "Mother is already gone. Please do me the favor and go find Wilford and let him know." And they also had to go look for my brother Guadalupe in Deer Creek. It was so difficult. There were no cars in those days. But we took my mother's body to the Whelan Ranch in a wagon, and my brother and father met us there in a truck. We had the vigil for her at the ranch. We lit candles and prayed the rosary all night long. Then the next day we took her by truck to Aravaipa and buried her in our family cemetery. Wilford arrived just as she was being buried; he had to come by horseback from so far away. It was not like it is today; there was no mortuary and people had to be buried the very next day after they died.

The day before, I had washed and combed her hair and trimmed her nails. And I had asked her, "Mama, how are you feeling?" "Believe it or not, I am feeling so good, hija, that I forgot all about the pills I'm taking." And she went out for a walk, and when I went to call her in for breakfast, there she was, singing—the cat following close on her heels. Who would have ever believed that she would die the very next day? It is hard for people to understand what we went through in those days. Everything seems so easy now. If you get sick, you just call the doctor on the phone. I felt so bad for such a long time after that. There were times when I didn't even know what was going on around me, when I didn't even realize I was crying. After that my sister Aurelia came to stay with me until the baby was born in May.

We had four children: Margaret, Harvey, Alicia, and Barbara. In those days there were parteras who delivered the babies. Livoria Moraga, the wife of Don Ignacio Moraga, was a very good partera. She delivered our first child, Margaret, at the 76 Ranch near La Bonita. She was already quite old by then. When I began to go into labor, my in-laws brought this woman to me. She greeted me and examined me. She said to Mamá Nacha (Nacha was the name of my husband's mother—I always called her

Mamá), "Ay, Nachita, you are very scared. But don't be afraid or worried." She stood at the foot of my bed and said, "Look me straight in the eye." "Look, Nachita," she said to my mother-in-law. "If she does not have the baby by one or two, then she won't have it until eight or nine o'clock." And the baby was born at ten minutes to nine, just as she had said. Doña Livoria stayed with me for five days, until it was time to cut the umbilical cord. She said, "I will not leave you. I birthed this child and I will stay, because I am responsible." And you should see how many babies that woman delivered!

One time, years later, I went to visit Doña Livoria in Willcox. She was very, very old. She was lying in bed in her little room covered up with a sheet. She didn't feel much like talking. She was not well. After a while she said to me, "Tell me, Rosa, do you still like to dance?" "Oh, yes," I told her. And that really amused that little old lady and she started to laugh.

I really don't understand how those parteras did what they did, but I had very good luck with them. And I say, if things went well with the first partera, then why change? My daughter Alicia was delivered by a midwife in the little mining town where we lived called Copper Creek. Her name was Doña Soledad Valenzuela. She was recommended to me. And Barbarita was delivered by a partera in Yuma named Doña Clarita Sánchez. My son, Harvey, is the only one who was delivered by a doctor—and another little girl that I had who died.

You are better off having your babies at home because if you have other children you can be there keeping an eye on them—what they are eating, what they're doing. You may be in bed, but you know what's going on!

After Wilford and I were married, we lived for a time at La Bonita. My husband worked mostly as a cowboy, but he could do almost anything. In those days a man did what he had to do to find work—ranch, farm, cook, mine. Wilford was very quick and very dependable. He worked at some small mines in the area, but they never lasted very long.

Then we moved up to Copper Creek, which is a small mining

town in the hills up above the San Pedro River. We were there about three years. How I loved that place! The people were so warm and friendly. I felt bad when we had to leave, but they closed the mine down after the owner died. The inspectors came and said that they were not using good quality wood for shoring up the tunnels, and the mine was dangerous.

During the Depression we came back to Aravaipa Canyon to help my father on the farm. Times were very hard; people went without clothes; they went without shoes. We didn't have any money, that's true, but at least we didn't go without food. It wasn't like in the cities where the people suffered so much they had to be in food lines! We had plenty of meat, plenty of eggs, plenty of milk. All we had to do was wait for the greens to come in the summer because frijoles we had! Sometimes when the men got work, they'd be paid with a calf or a heifer. I remember when a man named Juan Urías was paid with a load of hay. He said, "But I can't eat *hay!*"

We traveled a lot looking for work those early years we were married. Going from ranch to ranch. But we were always together. We went to Yuma, but we didn't like it there because they didn't give us a good house. We lived in Somerton quite a while. Wilford worked on a ranch and a farm.

After that my husband got a job at the Trench Mine in the hills above Patagonia. That is when we moved here. He loaded the ore from the mine to the train in Patagonia for it to be shipped out. It was dangerous work because that ore that he was breathing was black and dirty.

Then he left that job at the mine and came to work for Mr. Weatherhead. It was a better job. He was a man from Ohio who had bought some land here and had built a house. He used it as a dude ranch for his friends. Wilford was a "Man Friday." He was in charge of everything—the horses; taking the guests on rides; chauffeuring them all around, even across the line. Many times he didn't get home until one or two in the morning. He worked so hard that he suffered from nervous exhaustion! He worked for Mr. Weatherhead for nine or ten years.

Then he went to work as a cowboy at the Baca Float Ranch. It was owned by Jim and Talbert Pendleton. He worked there for thirteen years. There was a lot of land on that ranch—a lot of land! Now it's called Río Rico. It's all houses. When they first started building the houses, my daughter said to Wilford, "You should go over there and see those houses they're building!" He said, "I don't want to see them! Such wonderful land for raising cattle so that people can eat meat, and now they're building those horrible houses on it!"

Wilford stopped working at the Baca Float when he was thrown from that horse and injured. He was sixty-nine years old. He didn't want to quit working, but the doctors forced him to. They wouldn't allow him to ride anymore. He'd say, "My back and legs hurt, but when I get on a horse, they don't hurt me anymore!"

Wilford died in 1982 at the age of eighty-one. Oh, he was a good husband and not just because I'm saying it! His mother taught her sons to cook and wash because she said that if she wasn't around they could at least take care of themselves. He was very helpful with the children.

Part of our ranch in Aravaipa stayed in the family. When my father died, each of us girls got a parcel of land. My brother Guadalupe inherited the larger part of the ranch. My brother stayed and ranched in the El Cañón and lived there until he died in 1975. My other sisters—Victoria, Luisa, and Refugia—went away for short whiles, but they always returned. Victoria's son José still has some land in El Cañón, but he works in Dragoon and comes and goes. My brother's youngest son, Epimenio—we call him "Tex"—lives in Safford but also has a parcel of land there. He still has cattle there. Much of the property was sold to the Nature Conservancy, but they have leased some of it back. Now you need permission to go into the canyon.

The only one of the family who still lives there all year round is Victoria's granddaughter, Norma Luepke. She and her husband, John, live in the house that belonged to Victoria.

A lot of people go there now because there are a lot of places to camp and a lot of big trees and clean clear water. The last time we had a family reunion, there were all kinds of people camped under every tree!

I sold my parcel to my sister Lucía, and her children still own that. They're going to hang on to it because that is where their roots are; they don't intend to ever let it go. They might not have anything else, but they have the land.

Eva Antonia Wilbur-Cruce

M Y NAME IS EVA ANTONIA WILBUR-CRUCE. I was born on our ranch in Arivaca on February 22, 1904. My father, Augustín Wilbur, was the son of Dr. Ruben Augustín Wilbur, who was born in Boston, Massachusetts, and went to Harvard Medical School. When he finished medical school, he went to San Francisco with Charles Poston, and they came to Arizona to the Cerro Colorado Mining Mill in Arivaca in 1863. My grandfather was the doctor of the mining company and Charles Poston was the manager. Grandfather Wilbur's wife, my grandmother, was Rafaela Salazar, from Altar, Sonora. Her family had already moved to Arivaca, where he met and married her. Grandfather Wilbur homesteaded his ranch in Arivaca about a mile from the mining company. My father, the oldest of the three Wilbur children, was born on the ranch.

My mother's name was Ramona. She was the daughter of Don Francisco Vilducea, whose father was from Florence, Italy, but my grandfather was born in Mexico, somewhere around Alamos. He married Margarita López. Grandmother and Grandfather Vilducea left Mexico because my grandfather was being pursued by the government. They walked across the country with their children. I think it took them about three months to reach the creek at the Wilbur holdings.

They settled at the ranch and took over the house across the creek that had been built by Don Leonardo Suástegui. The two homes, those of my mother's and my father's parents, were across the creek from one another.

We grew up *encorralados*—fenced in. I had no social life whatsoever. The only friends I had were the Indians until they too left. My father did not allow us to go to school in Arivaca. It's very difficult to grow up like that; I was naturally very outgoing, and my father couldn't correct me because I would go around circles and come out with the same idea. I had my own ideas, and I would carry them out; he would often tell me, "Let nothing ever break your spirit." Nothing ever did!

My Aunt Mary, my father's sister, worked as a secretary for the Randolph offices in Tucson. She came to Arivaca to homestead a place adjoining ours, and she stayed with us for about six months while she was building her house. As soon as she settled down, she began to teach us. I was already six years old; she was our teacher for about six or seven years.

We had a building that was like a barn and in that big room they had put a plank on three boxes—one at each end and one near the center. Aunt Mary sat in the center, and I sat on one side and my sister Ruby sat on the other. The plank was about a foot wide and about fifteen feet long and was very close to the wall— twelve or eighteen inches away. It was a traumatic ordeal to sit so close to the wall, trying to study. Our days started at six o'clock in the morning, and we got out at twelve o'clock for lunch. At 1:00 P.M. we returned to class and we sat there until three o'clock when we got a fifteen-minute recess. Then we would return to the plank where we studied until six o'clock. In those days we had what we called a *pizarra*—a little slate. I would write on it, and then my aunt would give it to my sister.

It was difficult for me to learn to read. I didn't understand it because they used the old Spanish readers to teach us; the words were divided into syllables. First, there would be a group of all the CA words, like *casa* and *cantar*. And then all the BA's and so on. We would spell the letters and put the word together. For example, the word *vaca*. Be . . . A . . . (ba); Ce . . . A . . . (ca) . . . Vaca. Words like *queso* were very difficult because you had those three letters where the U is silent—Q . . . U . . . E. You had to learn Ku . . . U . . . E was *que* (kay) and SO was Ese . . . O (so). *Queso*. So when my father used to ask, "What did I say?" I used to answer, "You said, '*Ese oso*, Papa.'" And he would say, "We're not talking about *osos* (bears)! We're talking about *queso* (cheese)!" My father was teaching me one morning. I forget what word came up, but I said the wrong word and my father slapped the table. I ran out because I knew that when my father got angry he was *very* angry. And I ran into my friend Doña Tomaza's arms. She was looking for her horses down the creek. When she found out what was happening, she said that she would teach me how to read. She taught me that letters had names and

Augustín Wilbur, father of Eva Antonia, ca. 1930.

sounds, and she taught me how to put them together. I learned to read that very afternoon!

Aunt Mary used to give me very advanced work. I was reading *David Copperfield* before I could understand it. She used to tell my father, "She doesn't have a brain in her head."

I always loved to write but they didn't want me to write; they used to scold me, and I didn't know why. My father said to me, "If you want to starve to death, go ahead and become a writer."

One time I wrote a poem for my father, and even though he did not want me to write, when I showed it to him, he said, "That's good writing, Eva. I am going to show it to Mary." He took the poem to Mary and she had a fit. They had a big argument, and Mary closed up her house and called the cowboy. "Get me the surrey for tomorrow and take us to Arivaca. I want to go to Tucson." And they went and didn't come back until the following spring. She left because of that argument. She wanted me to be a bookkeeper, but I hated numbers.

My guess was that my father didn't get mad because I had put
him in the poem. Strange people! Ay! Ay!

In my dreams again
I see the little streams
That I used to cross
dashing
As I went splashing
To the opposite trail
Where I found and scared baby quail.
Slowly I went up the *colina* (hill)
Riding my beautiful Lina;
We went down the incline
Looking for what we call purple wine.
Somewhere in the deep gulch;
I found the purple moras growing in mulch
Their fruit was ripe and delicious,
And though the calls of the birds were vicious,
I ate to my heart's content,
And then up the hill again I went
To watch the fiery sunset sky
And herds of antelope going by.
This country was almost divine
And everything I beheld was mine.
The rolling hills, the lonely hills
Were covered in pink *guajillo* (fairy dust)
Clear up the mountains,
To the banks of the *río*.
Here in the lowland,
I gave Lina a free hand.
She took long, swinging strides
Which made more joyous my evening ride.
On the way back home I recrossed the stream,
Which made my life seem like a dream

From the gate Lina galloped to the kitchen door,
There stopping and refusing to go anymore.
When I petted her, I said to my father,
"She is my Lucky Seven."
And my father said, "And you, my daughter,
Are the star of my heaven."

I was trying so hard to write a poem. And my mother got all excited. "Look," she said. "Never say to people that you are writing poems, because you are not. A poet is a very highly educated man. You have never seen the inside of a school. People will think you are crazy. Say you are writing a story or something else, but don't say that you are writing poems." I said, "But, Mamá, I *am* writing poetry!" She said, "Don't talk like that! You are not!" So I decided, "Well, all right. I'll write *corridos* (songs). The cowboys write corridos, so why can't I?"

I remember one time when a flock of white-winged doves landed at the water hole where I was working. The white-winged doves had already hatched, but this flock of birds was late. I told my mother, and she said, "But it couldn't be!" "But it was, Mother! They came and landed with a breaking of mesquite branches." There was one little dove that stayed on the rock in the middle of the water hole. All the others flew away from me. My Aunt Rita had told me that when people caught these little birds for pets, they would cut off the fifth toe, and I noticed one toe was missing; so I decided that it was gentle, and it was. She stayed there, and I found it at the rock every time I went to the water hole. I wrote a corrido about the *palomita*:

PALOMITA PITAYERA	OH, LITTLE WHITE-WINGED DOVE,
Vente a dormir en mi higuera	Come and sleep in my fig tree
Abajo de mi ventana	Underneath my window.

Para verte muy ufana	So that I can see you, beautiful dove
En tu nidito mal hecho,	In your poorly made nest
En ese tu lecho,	Of breast feathers.
Duermes como en un templo	You sleep as if in a temple
Y me das el ejemplo	And you teach me
Con fe en el Creador	That in knowing God
Se retire el temor.	One loses fear.
Y cuando voy a orar	And when I go to pray
Y te oigo cantar,	And I hear you sing
Sé que somos dos espíritus	I know that we are one and the same spirit
Que venimos a Dios	That have come to worship
A adorar.	God.

I thought it was a great poem. I was crazy about writing. That's what I wanted to do. So one day my brother William, who was very young yet, was taken to a dance at the San Luis Mine by a cowboy. And the following day at breakfast William said, "I want to tell you something you will like, Bonnie." And I asked, "What, William?" And he said, "You know, at the dance last night they sang 'Palomita'!" I was so excited! Ecstatic! But no one spoke. No one approved. I walked away angry and disgusted. "Ay, Palomita, ay! If I could only fly!"

I was very young when my father told me, "When I go away, you are the boss and you are responsible. You tell the men what to do and see that they do it." So in the spring when the men were working on a fence, I had to go and stand there and tell them what to do and see that they did it. I guess my father chose me because I was the oldest, and he thought that I was more able to handle the job. But it wasn't true! My sister Ruby was more able than I. However, I had to ride and see what the men were doing. Sometimes they would sit down and smoke, and I would tell them to get on with their work. But it wasn't fun to be boss, you know. Mexican men are not bossed by women, especially in those days. And a little girl at that! They would say, "What's the

Eva Antonia dressed for work at age twelve.

matter with you? Are you crazy? Don't tell us what to do. We know what we're doing!" And I would go home and tell my mother, "Celso don't want to work, Ma." And my mother got on a horse and went with me. We stood on the hill and looked down at the men, and there was Celso working as hard as he could. My mother told him, "Bonnie says you don't want to work." And Celso said, "She's crazy, Señora. Ask my *compañeros* here and see if I'm not working. I've been working hard. All of us have. She doesn't know anything!" So it was very difficult for me. My father would get angry and say, "What happens there? Why can't you make the men work and not talk to you like that?" But I couldn't do any more as a child.

William and Ruby Wilbur, Eva's brother and sister, branding
cattle at the Arivaca ranch, ca. 1916.

One time my father went to see the fence they had made. He
pulled the top wire with a pulley and all the posts came up from
the ground. He said, "You're supposed to tell them how to do it."
And he got down from his horse and showed me how to put a
post down and tamp it so that when pulled, it didn't come out.

One time my father made us go and get the goats at night.
Some people think that it is easy to drive a herd of goats, but it is
not. A herd of goats is made up of old goats, mother goats, and
kids. And also young goats—three-, four-year-olds. When they
are driven the mother goats stop to nurse the kids, and the young
goats run off and separate from the herd. They have to be kept
together, and it's very difficult. So this time one goat was missing. My father came and stood before the herd of ten hundred
goats and asked, "Where's Pokey?" I said, "Papá, she didn't
come." "Why?" he said. "Well, I don't know. We lost her." Father said, "Hurry up; go and eat so you can go get her." It was
already getting dark. I said, "Well, we've already turned the
horse loose." Father continued, "The horse is not going to walk
over there; he didn't leave the goat. You did. You get ready and

walk up the mountain and get the goat." I don't know why Mother didn't object. The mountain was dark and dangerous. But she didn't. So Ruby said to me, "Hurry up, Bonnie. Get through eating so we can go and get the goat for Papá." I wanted to cry, but Ruby grabbed my hand and said, "Come on, let's go." We walked down on the trail along the bank of the creek. Ruby told me, "Look. If my father calls and you answer, I'm going to hit you over the head. Don't you dare answer him. Let *him* find *us*." And we crossed the creek at a sandy place and began climbing up the mountain. She said, "Make a beeline for the *peñasco*." The *peñasco* was a great big rock with a flat top. We used to walk up a mesquite tree and then jump down from the mesquite tree to the top of the rock. That's where we slept that night. My sister was very strong. I was two years older, but I followed her. That night there was a terrible noise—rocks rolling down the mountain—and we thought it was two men fighting. It turned out that two animals were fighting! This kept us awake all night. In the morning we went up the mountain and found the missing goat tangled in an ocotillo. By the time we untangled her, it was about eleven o'clock. On the way down the mountains we met one of the cowboys who said, "I told your grandmother that I saw you on the mountain last night, and boy, did your father ever get it!"

These are some of the things I had to do: I had to ride out of the fence into the National Forest to look for sick cattle. I would report their whereabouts and Father would go and find them and doctor them. I had to check the fences and see if they were down and report it. I was supposed to go and clean the water hole and see that the water was running well. If not, then my father would get a man to dig deep enough to bring the water up. I grew up doing these jobs from the time I was very young. The first two years I worked along the border. I was very resentful because I felt that I was the only girl in that country that was doing that kind of thing. It was a very difficult thing to accept. The water hole was maybe fifteen, twenty miles from the house, close to the border. As unpleasant as it was, I got in the habit of working alone, and when I got used to the animals and they got used to me, I wasn't alone anymore. They became good friends!

The ones I loved the most were the prairie dogs. They were very cute, and I always wondered why people don't take them for pets. I would feed the prairie dogs little pieces of jerky. When I first met them at the water hole they would run and hide and then come back one at a time. I would give them a little piece of meat, and the mother would come and look at it, change the morsel from one hand to the other, and then slap the little prairie dog and he would go rolling down. I used to be fascinated with their humanlike antics. They were darling little animals.

When I found the water hole was running good, I would just make a little ditch and let the water run and clean itself. Then I would have time to watch the animals. I would *take* time!

The Mexican hawk was another animal that I loved. One time when I got to the water hole, I found this hawk on the ground looking for water; the water hole was dry. I shoveled the sand where the water came out. The hawk lifted and flew up, but he stayed. He would come then whenever I was there. The second year, he was very friendly; he wasn't afraid of me. He would go right to the water hole; in the center there was a big rock where the hawk would sit and watch me work. I liked that. But when the hawk came, the little prairie dogs got scared and ran away into their dens, even when it was so hot. I felt sorry for them, so I used to throw water at the hawk, but I could never get rid of him. The only way that I could get rid of him was to sing. If I sang, then the hawk would fly up to the hackberry tree and north up to the trail and come back and fly over me, winging fast towards Mexico, where people knew how to sing. Very eloquent the animals are!

There were a lot of wolves in that country. My brother Henry was told to stay at the Cochis Ranch on the border when he was about seven years old. He slept there alone. He told me that a female wolf used to follow him, and he was afraid of her. I don't think that that female wolf wanted to hurt him; she could have hurt him if she wanted to. I believe now that she wanted to take care of him because he was small.

One time I went to the Cochis Ranch after I left the water hole. The ranch house was about three miles away. That morning when I left, I had told my mother that I was going to stay with Henry. When I got to the Cochis Ranch, it was beginning to get dark. My brother had already milked the cows and cooked supper. When we finished supper, he told me that he was going to make a bed for me by the window. I said, "Henry, I can sleep with you in the same bed." "No," he said, "I want you by the window because it's cool there." And he put a cot by the window and made the bed. He had those canvas cots that we used to open up called *tijeras* (scissors). I was just going to sleep when a wolf howled right by the window, which was just a hole in the wall. I jumped up and said, "Henry! Why did you put me by the window?" "Because," he said, "I wanted you to see what I go through every night!"

There were all kinds of animals. Deer, lots of deer. And bighorn sheep. Lots of raccoons and badgers, and burros, too. I used to count a thousand burros coming down the mountain. We don't have any now. And the mesquites were enormously big and round and tall.

These were my happiest years. The animals understood me and I understood them. I knew their language. They are terrific. I learned there alone what I didn't learn in school. I learned a little about brotherhood.

There were times when I would go up to the water hole and be so tired and sick. It was so hot. I would get under an oak tree where one branch had fallen and lay across it. I pressed hard against the tree and could feel something along my arms—a thumping. I thought, "What's doing this? Is it my body or the tree?" I felt some sort of nutrition coming from the tree. It gave me a lift; it gave me the stamina that I didn't have. I couldn't go anywhere or do anything but look at the blue distance. It spoke, and the wind sang and moaned. I learned to listen to the silence. When you are not alone, you sit and hear, but you don't pay attention to what you hear. When we are alone, ah, that's when we listen, and that's when we hear. We hear the wind sing and nature pulsate.

There was a mesquite tree that had a fork, and in the fork a big nopal was growing in a big crack. I suppose that the roots of the nopal made that crack. And there were great big prickly pear pads circled with the red tuna and a quail sitting on top of it! It was beautiful! I thought, "When I grow up I am going to be an artist and paint that mesquite with the quail and the red tuna." In that same place another tree with a fork fell on top of the mesquite that had the nopal and kept it from splitting up. So it spread out. I thought it was beautiful, too! It gave the impression that someone had propped it up.

One time when I was going over to check the water hole, my father told me, "If Luis Romero is there, give him this twenty dollars that I owe him so he won't have to come this way." Luis Romero came by in a wagon with some people who had bought or leased a place in the National Forest. They began to tear down the whole thicket of mesquite trees. The nopal came down, too, and they chopped it up. The foreman told me, "We're doing everything we can to preserve this country. You're going to see how nice it will be." The undergrowth was about waist high. He said, "The undergrowth is bad. You'll see. In twenty years the grass will be up above your stirrups. We'll put this fence here; it will be beautiful, straight like an arrow." But twenty years later, after I had gotten married, I took my husband up there to show him the country. The water hole was dry. There was no undergrowth. The rocks were bare against the soil. There was one bull standing under an oak, alone. They destroyed the whole thing! There was no water hole, no prairie dogs, no hawks, nothing. I walked away sick.

I had another experience in that country. We had a cowboy from Texas who was a government hunter. He used to trap for the pelts of coyotes and wolves. He had about two hundred pelts, and he sold them and bought himself a horse and an outfit—chaps and spurs and everything. He bought a horse from my father who was reluctant to sell him that particular horse because he could be thrown. But he said, "No. I'm not afraid. I am as able as any of your riders." So when we went down to the water hole, he went with us. Coming back, he reached up to an elderberry tree to pull down a little spray of mistletoe. The whole clump of mistletoe fell on the rump of the horse. The horse reared and the cowboy was thrown off. My father gave him *his* horse so he could go and hunt for the runaway and bring him back, but he couldn't find him. So the following day we went back to see if we could find the horse that had run away with the saddle and bridle. We trailed him to the place where we could see tracks that went up the bank and then disappeared. We called in the Buffalo Soldiers who were stationed at Arivaca, and they went over to see if they could locate him. But they said, "That horse went to Mexico."

Many years later I took my husband, Marshall, there to see the country. He went on one side of the wash and I on the other side up the mountain. When I got up to the top I waited. Looking down I saw him standing under an oak tree for what seemed a long time. Finally, he got on his horse and came up and was delighted with his find. "Look what I have," he said. "It's hardware of a saddle—the cinch rings, the bridle bit, the conchos!" "So where did you get that?" I asked him. "In the fork of that tree," he said, pointing to an oak. "There is a skeleton of a horse!" It was the skeleton of the horse that had been lost so long ago. I recognized the conchos of the bridle.

It was so difficult to grow up with the strict ideas of those days. I don't know whether it was just the Mexican people or everybody; the mores and morals were so old-fashioned. A woman would say to her daughter, "Look here, Panchita. When Roberto came in, you looked at him straight in the eye. I saw you *sin vergüenza* (shameless one). Cast your eyes downward; he'd think more of you if you did." But at least the "Panchitas" had contact with people in general. We had none. We were confined, restrained by my father's ideas, no arguments or questions asked. His iron will kept us silent and hoping for the years to set us free.

I grew up alone, but all of a sudden Father decided that a convent school was the best place for me. He took me to a convent in Los Angeles that had fifteen hundred girls. I think it was my Aunt Mary's idea; she went to the St. Joseph's Academy in Tucson. I had never seen the inside of a school until I went to this Guardian Angel School with the Sisters of Mercy when I was about thirteen years old. I thought I would die in that rodeo of

1916

Eva Antonia dressed for boarding school, ca. 1916.

people—never alone, always surrounded. I stayed there until they turned it into a military school for boys. My teachers went to Bakersfield and I went with them. I was with them about five years, until I was eighteen years old.

When I first went to this school, I would hide in the playroom where they had a piano. The piano was in a corner with enough space so that I could squeeze behind it and make myself comfortable. I used to stay there while music students visited with the music teachers. One day a girl came and said, "Well, Sister, what's the matter with Eva? What kind of a person is that? Where did she come from?" And the Sister said, "From someplace in Arizona—some wild place. I don't know where it is, but they eat chicken and spareribs with their hands, and they point at people. Horrible people! You must be kind to her because she doesn't know anything." And I sat there listening to every girl who came and talked, and I would guide myself by that.

They had a swing, and the girls would swing standing up and carry on a conversation across the fence with the gardeners who came to cut the grass. They made a great big pile of leaves in different parts of the garden. I went over to the fence, and I looked through the cracks and said to the man, "That smells good, that grass!" "Yes," he said, "sure." And I said, "Why don't you make the pile right over here so that I can see it." "Sure," he said. "We don't care. We can pile it anywhere." So he started piling the grass right where I wanted it, and I began to swing. I let go of the swing and landed on top of the pile of cuttings. I went up the hill through the wash to Mrs. Leona Chipley's house. She was a historian, and I used to recite to her the little poems I wrote when I was at the ranch. She was the first person who listened to me and encouraged me to write. She taught me lots of things that I didn't learn at the convent. She was from England, and I told her that I was from Arizona and that it was hard to be over at the convent alone. She said, "Well, you don't need to worry; just do your work." She taught me how to make cookies. She showed me all the books she wrote and suggested books that I could read.

Then I'd go back and wait until I heard the dinner bell. Then I'd jump over the wall.

I returned to the ranch in the summers. After the first year I was over the terrible nostalgia. I had already made a few friends, and I was looking forward to going back. For some reason or other, I made some friends that were good people. I don't know how I did it or why or how it happened. I went in September, and by April these girls would take me out with them. "When my mother comes, I'll ask her to take you." And so that's the way I learned the surroundings of the convent; I got to go out to different places.

I came back from the school around 1920. I connect the idea of change with my Grandfather Vilducea. "Everything," my grandfather used to say, "is a change. Life is a change. You have to accept it or you can't live." At that time my father was more Anglo than the Anglos. He never spoke to me in Spanish; he spoke to me in English. When I came back my father met me, speaking with a strong Spanish accent. I wasn't used to it. I said, "What's the matter with my Papá?" He said, "Well, I have ten Mexican families here, and that's all I speak. What do you want?" And when *I* came back from Los Angeles, I would have an English accent. Talk about a change! My mother spoke mostly Spanish, but she spoke English, too, mixed from beginning to end. What I speak is a corral dialect, a Wilbur dialect! In fact, my brother Henry told me once when I went to see him in Los Angeles: "When I came here, Eva, would you believe me that nobody understood me, except William, my brother?" Of course I believed him!

I returned just before the year of the Big Drought. That was in 1921. The cattlemen lost all their cattle. You used to go up on the hill by the road that goes to Arivaca, and you could smell the country—all the dead animals. All the cattle died, and we had to start back from scratch. We had very few cows and very few horses, but my father built it up again to about ten hundred head or so. But by that time my father had lost the Cochis Ranch. The soldiers that had been with Villa deserted the troops and formed gangs. They crossed the line and came to the Cochis Ranch, right on the border. One of them shot my father in the arm. After that my father told Henry, "See that you stay home; we'll do something else here." He just gave it up. He had to.

My father put me in charge again when he went to town. It was very unpleasant because I was now a woman. I would rather have gone into town, of course. I had already been in school, and I knew different things. I didn't care to go back to that old life I knew. The animals didn't know me anymore, either.

We would spend the whole day in the saddle, riding fifteen, twenty miles. We saddled the horses before dawn and had breakfast. We'd drive the cattle, horses, or goats, whatever. We'd move the cattle from the creek to the mountains and from the mountains to the creek. That took a long day and sometimes a day and a night. We'd get back after dark. There's a million things you have to do. If the cattle have maggots, or wounds and are in danger of getting maggots, then you rope them and doctor them.

*The Wilbur family in Arivaca, 1923. Ramona Vilducea Wilbur, Eva's
mother, with her children,* left to right, *Ruby, William, Henry, Eva
Antonia, and Mary.*

Then we'd bring in the milk cows every day, and my mother and
her helpers would milk them and make cheese. But driving the
cattle was the main part.

In those days we paid a dollar a head to keep the cattle in the
National Forest. The government would have roundups and
count the cattle of a certain brand. They'd turn the cattle loose
right there where they had the roundup. How far do you think
cows go at night? Fifteen, twenty miles! So the next day they
would have another roundup and round up the same cattle.
Sometimes they'd count the same cattle five times. So Ramón,
the Arivaca Cattle Company foreman, and my father and some
neighbors decided to get together and bring the cattle in before
the government started its roundup in the spring. That was steal-
ing their own cattle back, but what could you do? Later, they actually ran the cattlemen out of the National Forest. It was a fight

all the way. After they fenced the National Forest, you had to have a permit for so many cattle, and if they found one more than your permit allowed, then you were fined. So we brought our cattle to the creek in Arivaca and kept the herd down. In those days my father had fifteen sections.

As I told you, I didn't like this kind of life anymore. I was bored, but I did love to ride, so I would take my books, pencils, and my writing and get on my horse and go for the day.

One time I said to my mother, "I'm going to get on my horse today, and go for a long ride." Mother reminded me that it was June 24, San Juan's Day. Be sure that you come across the creek before 2:00 P.M., but if the flood should come before you get here, stay across the creek; don't try to cross." I said, "No, I'll be here by twelve o'clock." But as soon as I got on the horse I forgot all about San Juan's Day. I rode almost to the Cochis and back. I enjoyed looking at the country, the trees, the birds, and the trail. It was so fascinating.

The *chilipotle* is a plant that has a pod with red beans inside. As I sat breathing my horse, I heard a little popping noise. It was a chilipotle pod opening! It was satiny white inside with all those red beans clinging to the beautiful background. As I sat there I saw the cattle going to the water hole, and I wondered why there was water running down the side of the hill across the way. I went over to water the horse, but it was honey coming down the rock!

I stood on the mountain looking down. I saw a *churrea* (roadrunner) coming with a rattlesnake. The bird sat on a rock and began to eat it. I wondered how the little churrea could manage. It has a long tail, but it is a small bird and this was a big rattlesnake. She sat there eating, choking on it, swallowing it little by little.

With all these things, I forgot about the rains. All of a sudden the thunder came. I looked up, and there was a great big thunderhead! Walking on the mountain, I hadn't seen it. So I ran to the ridge to look down at the house. I could see a white curtain of rain. I went down, got my books from the tree, and turned to come back to the house. I thought to myself, "Even if I can't see, the horse will see." But the horse refused to go. He turned west and put his head down. The whole herd of goats was lying with their heads down, facing west, away from the storm. I remembered what my mother had told me: "In Rome, do as the Romans do." I put my head down and waited until the storm was over. I couldn't cross the creek because the water was from bank to bank, so I went over to a little wash that was not running anymore. There I saw the footprints of María, an Indian. María's big toe and little toe were spread out so I knew it was her. I hated her so much when I was a little girl. She used to sit for my mother. But when I saw that track, I was ecstatic! I waited there for a little while, wondering what I would do if she didn't come. It was cold, and I was soaking wet. I decided to make a ditch and lie down; the sides of the ditch would keep the air from me. And then María came. She said, "We're going to my place to sleep under the cottonwood." She had a place on the side of the bank under the roots of the tree. It was real warm, but it had a strong odor from the rats and mice. Before we went to the cottonwood María said, "We'll go over there to the ash tree so that your mother can see you across the creek." I thought she was very considerate to think of my parents. They went home knowing well that I was safe. I slept with María that night under the cottonwood tree.

Sometimes I hear Anglos say, "Oh, that's Mexican! It doesn't rain on San Juan's Day!" But *I* know it does!

My father died in April 1933. He had an aneurysm caused by the kick of a horse. Many years later he was thrown from a horse and when he fell, the aneurysm burst. They immediately brought him to Tucson, but when he got to the hospital the doctors said he was dying. At that time I was in Los Angeles, going to Woodbury College. It was a two-year course, but I was in my third year because those were difficult times and I had to work. I worked for the Eastern Outfitting Company, and I didn't want to quit because I was learning as I worked and getting experience. I also worked for the Farmers and Merchants Bank in Los Angeles, but in 1933 I came home again and never went back.

I arrived during the wake at my Aunt Carlota's home. I walked in and saw the coffin in front, and one of the ladies said,

"There is Eva Antonia, poor thing. I hope that she is smart enough to go back and not stay." Another lady said, "Oh, she'll go back. Don't worry."

After the funeral, Pancha, an old woman from Arivaca, said to me, "You know, your father and one of the cattlemen over there were having a cattle war. You'd better go back to Los Angeles, because you're going to be in the middle of it. If you get in there, you're going to get it." I thought to myself, "Well, it isn't my cattle war. I have nothing to do with it. Why should I get it?" So I stayed. And I got it! My brothers went away; my two sisters also got married and went away, and I was left alone with a cattle war on my hands.

Cattle wars are about land and water. In a cattle war people kill each other's stock or they kill each other, if they possibly can. You can imagine how hard it was for me. I was alone and a woman. My brother Henry came one day and said, "I have to look for the horses." We found eight horses dead in a ravine. We reported it to the sheriff's department, and the officers went over and found horses all over the country—dead. Mr. Post, the ranger over in Arivaca, told me that he had seen a man get a machine gun and kill ninety-six saddle horses.

People are wrong when they think I inherited the ranch. No, I bought it. When the estate was closed, Judge Hall called me and said, "Now the ranch is for sale." He wrote a letter to every one of the heirs. Nobody answered. The judge asked me, "Why haven't they answered?" And I said, "I'll ask them." They said, "We've had enough of ranching, thank you!" But I wanted to keep the ranch, so I went to Bernabe Robles and borrowed the money. I think it was about fifteen hundred dollars. "I want you to know, Eva," he said, "that I'm lending you this money because of your father." I didn't care why he loaned it to me as long as he gave me the loan. We had an awfully hard time paying Robles back, but we finally did.

After my father died, I met my husband Marshall. I met Marshall in the fall after my father died, on a Saturday, and we married on Monday, November 19. We had a wonderful rela-

Eva Antonia Wilbur-Cruce and Ruby Wilbur Zimmerman after a cattle inspection at Figueroa Ranch, April 24, 1941.

tionship. We have been married fifty-six years! Right away we bought a lot from DeConcini on East District and built a house. My husband worked for Carl Hayden Hospital for a long time. Later on he was a shipping clerk at Montgomery Ward's. While he was at work, I hauled the soil, I hauled the sand, I hauled the rocks, and then I hired a young boy to help make the adobes. We built a one-room house without a door or windows.

I used to wake up in the morning and there would be a snake under the bed. At one time, before I built the house, we camped there with a tent. My sister said, "I'd rather raise my kids under a mesquite tree than live like that!" Nobody had ever built a house like that! The door was so bad—leaning this way and that—that I propped it up with a board. But I finally made it livable. I was comfortable. I had my radio, my telephone, but I never received people.

We had to do that in order to keep the ranch. We spent every weekend there, but the ranch went down. It was not easy to leave the place alone and find it the way we had left it, especially during the Depression. Cattle are edible, and people had to eat. It was bad. Everyone took what they wanted.

I used to have a cowboy—one of the López boys—who would go out there and help me. We had the cattle then; but about 1940 we sold all the cattle. We still had the horses, and we *still* have them. It is an old herd; they are descended from the Spanish mustangs that were brought in the 1800s from Rancho Dolores in Mexico. We would sell a horse now and then. And my husband had beehives, about fifty, and he sold the honey. We also sold wood, and we had a nursery business, too. Sometimes we would spend months out there potting plants in tin cans under the cottonwoods. Back then you could buy plants when they were small and sell them when they were bigger at quite a profit.

When I sold the ranch to the Nature Conservancy, I kept the house and ten acres. We have the house and the hill and it joins the road where that comes in. The creek is lovely. The big cottonwoods remind me of happier days. A woman called me the other day and wanted to know if she could buy our whole herd of wild mustangs and not separate them. I'll let them have the horses if they do that. I like that.

The other day I was thinking of a funny story about my sister Ruby and my brother William. We had no toys, and we never played with dolls. We played with cattle! We had bones. The big bones were the cows and the little bones were the calves. I had mine and my sister Ruby had hers, and we made corrals with little stones. One day I came in and said to William, "Look. My cow hasn't got a calf. Why?" And Ruby said, "Tell her that you stole the calf." William said, "I stole it." And I said, "Ruby, you're the inspector. What should I do?" Ruby said, "Hang him!" I said, "But you're the inspector. Come and help me." We had a little white cotton rope, and we pulled him up in a tree. It's a wonder we didn't kill him! That night at dinner William said to my father, "Those bitches hung me." My father got the strap that was hanging on the wall and said, "You know, if you talk like that about your sisters, you're going to get it." At the same time my father noticed William's neck was all red, and he said, "William, what's wrong with your neck?" William said, "I'm telling you! They put a rope around my neck and pulled me up a tree!"

I still have one of those *huesitos* (little bones) at the house that I have saved. It was there by the telephone at the house on East District. I hope it is still there.

Editor's note: Eva Antonia Wilbur-Cruce is the author of *A Beautiful, Cruel Country*, which chronicles her life in Arivaca up to the age of six (University of Arizona Press, 1987).

Carlotta Silvas Martin

MY NAME IS CARLOTTA SILVAS MARTIN. I was born in Superior, Arizona, on December 4, 1917. My father's name was Miguel López Silvas. He was born in Imurís, Sonora, Mexico, on May 17, 1888. My father's parents, Petra López and Jesús Silvas, died when he was just two years old. My father was the youngest of seven children and was raised by his older brothers and sisters. He went from pillar to post and was never sent to school. He grew to manhood unable to read or write, and he regretted that all his life. He used to tell me, "Si yo hubiera tenido madre, yo hubiera ido a la escuela." ("If I had had a mother, I would have gone to school.")

My father came across the border to Arizona many times in his teen years; at that time there was no immigration office. He worked on farms and ranches as a laborer; he was a very hard worker. He told me of the summer that he spent in Safford working on the farms of the Mormon people. The hours were long, the work backbreaking. He spoke of their kindness to him. They would set a table brimming with food and insist that he sit and share the meal with them.

My father met Santiago Jórquez in Safford, and the two remained lifelong friends. In 1911 they came to Superior to look into the possibility of working for Magma Copper Company. They decided to return to Safford, and they worked for the railroad for a time. The pay was one dollar for a ten-hour shift. From this meager wage my father sent money to his sister Francisca in Nogales.

In 1913 my father returned to Superior and was hired as a miner by Magma Copper Company. He became a boarder at Josefa's Boarding House, which belonged to my maternal grandmother, Josefa Tapia. That is where he met my mother, Elena Amanda Romero. My mother lived in Florence with *her* grandmother and came to Superior from time to time to visit her mother and brother.

My mother was born in Florence, Arizona, on July 26, 1895. Her parents' names were José María Romero and Josefa Tapia. My maternal grandfather was born in a small village near Imurís,

*Josefa Tapia, musician and maternal grandmother of Carlotta
Silvas, ca. 1890. Josefa raised Carlotta.*

Sonora, Mexico. My maternal grandmother was born in a tiny
settlement near Florence called Sanford; it doesn't exist anymore.
The marriage of my grandparents broke up while my mother
and her two brothers, Ernesto and Arturo, were quite young.
My grandfather returned to Mexico, and my grandmother eventually moved to Sonora, Arizona, with the two boys. Sonora was
a community populated by Mexican families who worked for
Kennecott Copper Company. In 1911 my grandmother decided
to move to Superior where the Lake Superior and Arizona Mine
and the Silver Queen Mine provided work for a large number of
miners. My grandmother and my mother's brothers, now in
their teens, hitched their only horse to a wagon and piled it with

a crate of chickens and a few possessions. A pet bull, raised by my two uncles, was tied to the back of the wagon. The family dog trotted alongside the wagon on the two-day trip to Superior; when he tired, he was put into the wagon to rest.

When they arrived in Superior, my grandmother set up a makeshift tent of clapboard and canvas on a narrow strip of land next to where the Queen Creek Bridge now stands. It was left of the present Superior Fire Department and opposite of La Olla Motel. She filed a claim and the land eventually became hers. In those days, a person could settle wherever he or she wanted.

My grandmother's homesite, as I said, became a boarding house—a three-meals-a-day eatery for the miners. She cooked on a wood stove and had log benches and tables. Many Mexican women did that for a living in those years. There were a lot of miners coming in and no facilities for food or lodging. My grandmother used to tell me that people were even living in caves, in dugouts on the sides of the hills that had been previously occupied by Apache Indians.

The family of Antonio and Edubiges (Vicky) Santa María lived in one of those caves. María Pacheco,* their daughter, was telling me about it the other day. Her father built an adobe room at the entrance to the cave. The cave itself was quite large and divided into rooms by wooden partitions. Sr. Santa María built a stone building outside which he used as a bakery, and Sra. Santa María had a beautiful flower garden. María's mother was another very enterprising woman of that era. She made and sold food; she sewed dresses for the Apache women; she taught reading and writing for lessons. She was also a *curandera*. There were just company doctors in those days, and people depended on Sra. Santa María to cure them of their ailments. She raised her own

*María Santa María Pacheco was born in Silverbell, Arizona, on February 10, 1905. Her mother, Edubiges Valles Santa María, was born in Visalia, California, in 1879, the daughter of Leonardo and Leonora Valles. The maternal grandparents of Edubiges had gone to California from Sahuaripa, Sonora, with the intention of beginning a business during the Descubrimiento (Gold Rush Days).

Elena Amanda Romero and Miguel Silvas, parents of Carlotta, at Superior, Arizona, 1917.

medicinal herbs and also gathered them in the mountains and desert. She was also a *partera*; she delivered many of the babies in the town.

My mother and father were married in March of 1917. My father bought an adobe house at 53 Pinal Street. It had just two rooms—a kitchen and a bedroom—and dirt floors. My sister Petra still lives in the family home. The address is the same, but they have done extensive remodeling.

All of us children were born in that house. I was born in December 1917, and Petra was born the following December, 1918. My sister Sophie was born in 1922. Our little brother, Miguelito, was born after Petra, but he died of intestinal fever. My father often spoke of his son and told me that when he died it was the most anguish he had ever felt in his life. He never got over it.

My mother had two small babies on her hands. When I became sickly, Grandmother Josefa took me home with her, and I never returned to my parents. From the time I can remember I was raised by my "Nani." In those years it was very common for grandmas to raise kids.

My grandmother worked very hard; I grew up during the Depression. My kids asked me why I can't ride a bike and I'd say, "That's the last thing I would ask for!" During the Depression my grandmother would give Armida, my Uncle Ernesto's wife, a dollar a day. With that she'd buy potatoes, lard, and beans. They had thirteen children, and she'd feed us all. That was the menu—*papas fritas*, *frijoles*, and *tortillas*. Aunt Armida made big piles of hot tortillas and we sat on those long benches and she gave them to us as she made them. Every once in a blue moon she bought a quarter's worth of hamburger and fried it with potatoes. That was a real treat!

During the Depression my grandmother sewed piecework for the WPA. I'd go by the building on my way to and from school and see her sitting at the sewing machine. My dad helped when he could, but the miners only made four dollars a day. Uncle Ernesto worked also. He used to dig graves.

My mother was very kind; she was known for her charity. She gave people food during the Depression. My dad used to buy one-hundred-pound sacks of sugar, flour, and potatoes, and my mother would portion it in little bags and give them to the people who were in need.

When my mother's father died, Doña Isabel, who never went out anywhere because she was partially paralyzed, went to my grandfather's wake. Mother asked her, "Ay, why are you coming out in this cold and windy weather?" "Because, Elena," she answered, "I owe you favors. If I owed you money, I would pay you, but I can only repay the kind favors that you have done for me by accompanying you in your grief." Many of the people in our little mining town were very ethical and high-class people in their own way.

Another young man was telling me the other day: "Carlotta, I never liked Superior because I suffered so much hunger there, but your parents were always very kind to us." "Yes," I told him. "They were kind to everybody."

The Depression years were very, very hard. I remember

seeing the people passing on the way to California from Okla-
homa, Arkansas, and Missouri. At that time we lived on Queen
Creek, and everyone went by there. It hurt me to see the people
in their rickety old cars, their clothes in tatters, escaping from the
drought and the dust bowls.

My grandmother was not a very religious person, but she did
the best she could. She sang in the church choir for many, many
years; she also played the organ there occasionally, and she played
the guitar and piano. She was very talented musically. She taught
herself to play the piano, and when she was older she took lessons. We had a very humble home, but I don't remember when
we didn't have a piano. It was old and beat up, but it had good
tone. She played waltzes and tangos like "Choclo," "Tango Ne-
gro," and "Queja Palmera." "El Choclo" had very complicated
fingerwork; she memorized the music. She played and sang some
of the "oldies" like "Ojos Tapatios" and "Morir Sonando." She
had a beautiful voice.

OJOS TAPATIOS

No hay ojos más lindos en la tierra mía
Que los negros ojos de la tapatia.
Miradas que matan
Ardientes pupilas
Noche cuando duermen
Luz cuando miran.

En noche de luna, perfume de azahares
En el cielo estrellas, y tibios los aires.
Y allí tras la reja
Cubierta de flores
La novia que espera
Temblando de amores.

Y al ver esos ojos
Que inquietos esperan
Apagan las luces

Las blancas estrellas.
Los aires suspiran aromas mejores
Y todas las flores suspiran de amor.

Por una mirada de tan lindos ojos
Estrellas y flores padecen enojos
Los aires suspiran
El cielo se apaga
Y en el alma vaga
La queja de amor.

TAPATIO EYES

The most beautiful eyes in my land
Are the dark Tapatio eyes.*
A glance from the burning pupils
Can destroy you;
They are like night when they sleep
And brilliant when awake.

On a perfumed and moonlit night
With a star-filled sky and warm breezes
There behind the window grill covered in flowers
The waiting sweetheart trembles with love.

Upon seeing those eyes that wait so impatiently,
The light of the white stars dim;
The air sighs with beautiful aromas
And all the flowers sigh with love.

The stars and flowers are jealous
Of such beautiful eyes;
The breezes sigh; the skies darken
And the love's complaint
Invades the soul.

*Refers to a person from the Mexican state of Jalisco.

The fraternal organizations like the Alianza Hispano Americana, the Woodsmen of the World, and the Porfirio Díaz put on dances, and my grandmother played the piano at some of those events. She could follow the orchestra with nothing but chords; that is very difficult and going out of style.

My early childhood years were spent playing in Queen Creek near my grandmother's home. It was so pretty—a green oasis shaded by huge cottonwood trees that made my playground a cool haven. Clean, clear water ran in the creek all the time. Sometimes, after a heavy rainstorm, the creek would flood as high as the bridge and then miraculously turn into a trickle the very next day. But now it's dirty, and there are no trees. My grandmother's house was located on the "American" side of town, but there was nothing they could do about it because she was there before anybody else and had staked her claim. Later on she sold the lot for five hundred dollars and moved the lumber and built another house on a lot she had on Heiner Street. I grew up playing with Anglo children and speaking English. Most of my friends were the Mahoneys, a big Irish family from Utah.

When it was time for me to go to school I was assigned to Harding School, which was the school for the non–English-speaking children on the Mexican side of town. We were segregated; there was a place called McKelveyville by Harding School, and those Anglo children were sent to Roosevelt School and the Mexican children who lived closer to Roosevelt had to go down to Harding. I'll admit, there was a lot of discrimination in those years. An ice plant located just below the present Hing's Market on Main Street seemed to be the unofficial boundary between the "American" side (we were all Americans!) and the "Mexican" side.

Superior's Mexican side of town could have been considered a barrio, but to me it was a lovely environment. The people were very united; they intermingled a lot. There was never a need to lock doors. I don't ever recall my seeing a key to any of the doors in either my parents' or grandmother's homes.

My mother practiced the traditions of Mexican culture. Christmas was the season she loved best of all; I can remember walking into the house and hearing her sing Christmas carols in Spanish as she worked in the kitchen. "Silent Night" was her favorite—"Noche de Paz, Noche de Amor."

I remember especially Las Posadas at Christmas. Las Posadas are a reenactment of the travels of Joseph and Mary who are looking for shelter before the birth of Jesus. Large groups of men, women, and children walked in procession through the darkened streets carrying candles. There were no street lights then. I was about five years old, and I remember hanging on to my mother's skirts because I was scared of the dark.

My friend María Pacheco was reminding me the other day of how during "Las Posadas" the young unmarried girls used to get dressed as angels in white robes made of gauze. They tied the gown at the waist with a cord and carried a shepherd's staff. The crook was decorated with paper flowers, and the one who had the most beautiful staff won a prize.

We'd arrive at a designated house and sing songs asking for *posada*, or lodging. The interior of the house was dark and those inside would answer that there was no room. We'd go to several houses until we arrived at a chosen house that would accept the pilgrims. Then we'd go in and have food—chocolate and *pan de huevo* (sweet eggbread) and a piñata full of candy. Often there was a decorated home altar with the nativity. The singing continued and the adults had the velación and said the rosary, and soon all of us kids stretched out and fell asleep right there on the floor.

This went on for nine nights—it was a *novenario*. On the twenty-fourth, the last night, we ended up at the church, and everyone stayed there all night for the vigil. We had gifts as well as a piñata. What a treat it was to get any little thing like that.

Here are a few verses of the "Las Posadas" that we used to sing:

PIDIENDO POSADA

Quien nos da posada
A nuestros peregrinos

Que vienen cansados
De andar los caminos.

Venimos rendidos
Desde Nazarét
Yo soy carpintero
De nombre José.

En nombre del cielo
Os pido posada
Pues no pude andar
Ya mi esposa amada.

(Rechazo)
Por más que digáis
Que venís rendidos
No damos posada
A desconocidos.

No me importa su nombre
Déjenme dormir
Pues que ya les digo
Que no hemos de abrir.

(Recibimiento)
Posada os damos
Con mucha alegría
Entra José justo
Entra con María.

Entren santos peregrinos, reciban este rincón
No de esta pobre morada, pobre morada,
Sino de mi corazón.

(ASKING FOR LODGING)

Who will give lodging to these pilgrims
Who are so tired from their journey.
We are exhausted from traveling from Nazareth.

I am a carpenter named Joseph.
In the name of heaven I ask you to give us lodging.
For my beloved wife can journey no longer.

(Rejection)
No matter what you say,
We'll not give lodging to strangers.
It matters not what your name is;
Let me sleep.
I've told you we will not open the door.

(Acceptance)
We will give you lodging with much joy.
Enter, oh just Joseph,
Enter with Mary.
Enter, holy pilgrims
Not into this humble dwelling,
But into my heart.

Then we'd sing many more songs; María Pacheco sang one to me
the other day:

Señor en la gloria
En Belén está
Cantando victoria
Vamos para allá.

Cuando lleguemos
Cuando vayamos y veamos
A Dios en aquel portal
Cantando todos
Llegamos para allá.

The Lord is in his glory in Bethelehem.
Victory we sing and journey there.

When we go there and see God in his portal,
We will arrive singing his glory.

We also had our Christmas at home. My mother made dozens and dozens of tamales by herself. I wonder now how she did all that; she didn't have a blender for the chiles or a mixer to beat the masa. She made buñuelos. She filled up a blue-gray enamel roaster and covered them with a dish towel. She made *miel de panocha* (syrup) with brown sugar and cinnamon; we'd pour it over the buñuelos. She made biscochuelos and teswín. It made us quite tipsy!

These special foods were also made for birthdays and saints' days. There would be serenades—"Las Mañanitas"—before dawn. How I remember the giggling as we stumbled around before dawn to surprise the celebrant!

Saints' days were very special—August 15 was my mother's saint's day; March 19 was the saint's day of her comadre Josefina; and December 12 was for the Guadalupañas. People didn't bring gifts; they brought real elaborate and romantic cards.

But they didn't have to have a saint's day to get together; there was a lot of socializing. We always had a lot of people at our home. My mother's comadres would come over to our house and cook a lot of food. They'd set the table outside because there was not enough room in the house. As regular as clockwork, the men were served first. Then they'd go off and sit around and talk and smoke. Then us children were fed. The ladies served themselves last and sat down and ate and talked and laughed while we played. It was very oriented toward family and friendship.

There was a strong feeling of community among the Mexican people of Superior. The fraternal organizations had socials and picnics as well as dances. When someone died, they all turned out in their uniforms and banners—all very formal.

We also celebrated Las Fiestas Patrias—el 16 de septiembre, el 5 de mayo, and also July 4. Some men in town knew a great deal about Mexican history and politics, and they were very involved in these celebrations. We'd have patriotic speeches, a queen and princesses, a parade with floats, a dance, and a picnic with races

Carlotta Silvas Martin, Superior, Arizona, 1936.

and pie contests. On September 16 they'd blow up some dynamite, and the blast would represent "El Grito de Dolores," which
was the cry for independence from Spain by Miguel Hidalgo.

We had a theater at one time in Mexican town. It had a very
nice stage and seated about three hundred people. It burned down
and was never rebuilt. Touring stock companies came from Los
Angeles and presented beautiful plays in Spanish—comedies,
dramas, and musical reviews. You know who used to come
here—Rita Hayworth! Her name was Rita Cansino then. She
toured with her father. They sang together and she danced. That
was in the early thirties.

I belonged to a women's group called "Las Mexicanitas." We
did a lot of community service. We raised money for scholar-
ships; we donated the altar and railing when they built the new
St. Francis Church and raised money for the St. Mary's Community Center. We put on plays and skits and variety shows. One

year I wrote a play in Spanish and English called "The Apparition of Our Lady of Guadalupe." Martin Fierro, the high school Spanish teacher, did the men's voices, and I did the women's voices. My husband, Walter, and I went up to the flats and collected manzanita bushes. Walter put them on stands, and we decorated them with paper roses. Then we blacked out the stage lights, and when the lights were turned on the Virgen de Guadalupe was standing there. Everyone said, "Ahhhhhhh." It was so beautiful. It was such a big success we had to put it on twice.

The first movie theater was in American town. Later we also had a movie house in Mexican town that had movies in Spanish. That's about the only time my mother would go out. How she enjoyed those movies!

My father was a very honorable man; his word was his bond. He was a very hard worker and was respected. Some of the men didn't like to work with him because he was such a perfectionist at his job. At one time he was a contract miner and worked in a very lucrative spot. He was a good provider. But then, that's not all there is to life. He was in charge of the money, but my mother had to save for any of the extras. Sometimes he would just blow it away. When he retired in 1950 he had worked for the mining company forty-three years and had never been laid off. If he went out and drank, which he did do, he'd go to work the next day. People would tell time by him. He had a lunch pail with a canvas strip that he swung on his back. By six o'clock every morning, he was going up the hill on Pinal. People would say, "Ay, ya son las seis. Allí va el Mique Silvas." (Oh, it's six o'clock; there goes Mikey Silvas.)

The miners worked very, very hard; they worked under intolerable conditions. It was very hot underground; it could get up to 140 degrees. There was no air conditioning like there is now. The dynamite blasts and the equipment down there stirred up dust. I remember when he came home he looked so terrible, so exhausted and tired, that his eyes would slip back into his head. A lot of miners were killed in that era. As recently as May 1966, three miners were killed in a dynamite blast caused by a short fuse. Their names were Joe Díaz, Frank Ruiz, and a Mr. Thompson. A corrido was written about it.

Almost all of the miners of my dad's era died of silicosis; silica is a very fine glass dust that gets into the miners' lungs. Eventually it digs a hole in the lungs. It's a very wasting disease. There was a lot of anger. They couldn't breathe, they coughed up blood, and they choked on blood. It was a horrible way to go. Many of the wives of the old-timers took care of their husbands. By the time they died, the wives were ready to die from exhaustion.

When my dad retired, he already had the disease. The mining company had a law that you had to have been underground within the last ten years, and my dad had been working above ground in the change rooms where the miners took their baths. The company used that as an excuse not to pay him his silicosis compensation of $2200. My dad didn't know how to speak English, so when the Labor Relations Board met, I went and gave them a piece of my mind. I said, "My dad has silicosis. Now where in the world do you think that he could have gotten it other than underground? He hasn't worked anywhere else." Eventually, he did get his compensation, but they cut off his $17 a month pension because they said that no one could receive two benefits at the same time.

I don't think I'm the one that scared them. At that time the union was trying to get in. Their meetings were held in secret. There were no death benefits for the families of the miners, no job protection. My dad never wanted to join the union, because during the Depression when the other mines were closing, Magma stayed open. They allotted each of the miners so many days' work so they could at least have some income. My dad felt a sense of loyalty to the company, and some of the other old-timers said, "We think Mique is right; we have to show our appreciation." But when they wouldn't give him his silicosis compensation, the union fought for him and got in right away. The old-timers said, "If they'll do it to Mique, they'll do it to anybody."

Matias Pacheco, María's husband, was very active in the union movement here; he was very progressive. He was born in Dos Cabezas, was an American citizen, and spoke English. He had been involved in the strikes in Cananea. He used to argue with my dad. "Look, Mique," he'd say, "don't be naive. You are being taken advantage of because you don't speak English."

My father died of silicosis in 1964 at the age of seventy-six. He had always been a strong man, and I am sure that he would have lived much longer if it hadn't been for that. He was in the hospital, and I thank God for that. Dr. John McAdams, a company doctor, took excellent care of him. He told us about the Bennet machine that cleared the phlegm out of the passages of the lungs. We rented one. So at least my dad was more comfortable towards the last than most. Dr. McAdams was let go by the company eventually because he cared more about the miners than the business end of the company.

As I told you, my dad's biggest regret was that he never learned to read or write. "Because of that," he said, "I have to work with my hands." So education was very important to him; he thought it was the one thing that would help us succeed. He always told us, "Now respect your teachers, because your teachers are like your second parents. Don't talk back to them, because if I hear about it I am going to spank you." We didn't have any trouble in school because he wouldn't have put up with it.

I found school very enjoyable. I loved English literature and history. I had a flair for writing. When I was in the fourth grade, I won the writing contests. One day our class wrote a letter asking about the tonnage that Magma was producing. My letter was chosen as the best one and was sent to the general manager. He wrote me a letter back. My dad was so proud of that letter. I think he kept it until the day he died. After I finished elementary school, I attended Roosevelt Middle School and then eventually graduated from Superior High School. I was the only Mexican girl to graduate from high school that year. It never occurred to me not to go to high school; my grandmother would get me up every morning and send me. The cold wind blows so hard here;

I remember walking backwards up the hill to school so the wind wouldn't hit me in the chest.

I attended Arizona State University for a couple of semesters but came home because I caught pneumonia; the dormitories were out in the open. I worked in a photography store and then in John Mitchell's Department Store for a number of years. I started writing feature stories for the *Superior Sun* newspaper in 1960 and worked for them eleven years. I wrote a social column called "Aquí y Allá" (Here and There). It covered baptisms, weddings, and the like. It was quite popular.

I married my husband, Walter Martin, in 1955. He is an Alaskan native and a mining engineer. We have two children, a son, Jonathan, and a daughter, Elena. I moved to Mesa for sixteen years so my children could attend school there. Our daughter is a music teacher at Lehi Elementary School in Mesa, and our son is a surveyor for Magma Copper Company.

I moved back to Superior three years ago, but so much has changed since the mine closed down in 1984. John Mitchell's was a beautiful department store with quality merchandise. There were appliance stores, two drugstores, and some nice restaurants. The Magma Hotel was a very nice place; the theater was going full blast. Every two weeks when the miners got paid, there was money flowing all over the place. It was a thriving town, and now it is barren, like the desert. Even the Kress' Dime Store has closed, and that was the meeting place for people.

I used to go and visit people that I have known since I was a little girl, but now so many of the people have gone away or died. I hardly go out anymore. To me that's one of life's sadnesses—to lose the people you've known all your life.

A lot of the children of the Mexican families from Superior have done very, very well. A lot of professional people have come out of our little mining community—doctors, lawyers, educators, and political leaders. A professor at ASU told me that young people from the mining towns always did well because they had support of their parents.

My sister's son, Aaron Kizer, is an attorney. I remember once when Aaron was a little boy he was singing "Anything you can do, I can do better." When my dad heard him singing that song, he asked me, "¿Que está cantando el muchacho?" I explained it to him. He got such a big kick out of that. He'd be so thrilled today if he knew how well our children have done.

Index

About the Author

PATRICIA PRECIADO MARTIN is a native Arizonan and a lifelong Tucsonan. She is an honors graduate of the University of Arizona. She has been active in many facets of the Mexican American community of Tucson and for ten years has devoted her time to writing, the collection of oral history, and the development of the Mexican Heritage Project at the Arizona Historical Society.

Her first book, *The Bellringer of San Augustín* (1980), is a bilingual children's book published for the International Year of the Child. Her first collection of oral history was *Images and Conversations: Mexican Americans Recall a Southwestern Past*, published by the University of Arizona Press, and it won in 1983 the Virginia McCormick Scully award for the best book of history by a Native American or Chicana. She has also written a book of short stories entitled *Days of Plenty, Days of Want*.

The author and her husband, Jim, whom she met while serving in the Peace Corps, have two college-age children. Although the author still lives in Tucson, she says, "I have left my heart in Aravaipa Canyon."